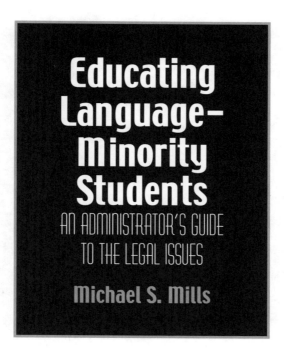

Educating Language-Minority Students

AN ADMINISTRATOR'S GUIDE TO THE LEGAL ISSUES

Michael S. Mills

Foreword by
Charles W. Goldner, Jr.

PHI DELTA KAPPA
EDUCATIONAL FOUNDATION
Bloomington, Indiana
U.S.A.

Cover design by
Victoria Voelker

All rights reserved
Printed in the United States of America

Library of Congress Control Number 2002114300
ISBN 0-87367-846-X
Copyright © 2003 by Michael S. Mills
Bloomington, Indiana U.S.A.

TABLE OF CONTENTS

Foreword v

Introduction 1

**Chapter One: A Ready Reference to Principles and
  Legal Requirements** 7
  OCR Compliance Reviews 10
  Need for a Program 11
  Program Adequacy 13

**Chapter Two: A Recent History of Language Policy
  in the United States** 17

Chapter Three: A Compendium of Court Decisions .. 25
  Meyer v. State of Nebraska 25
  Bartels v. Iowa 27
  Arvizu v. Waco Independent School District 28
  Lau v. Nichols 29
  Serna v. Portales 31
  Morales v. Turman 33
  Otero v. Mesa 34
  Aspira v. New York 36
  Alvarado v. El Paso Independent School District 37
  Armstrong v. O'Connell 38
  Cintron v. Brentwood 40
  Rios v. Read 43
  Guadalupe Org. Inc. v. Tempe Elem. Sch. Dist. 44
  Deerfield v. Ipswich Board of Education 46
  Martin Luther King Jr. Elem. School Children et al.
     v. Ann Arbor School Dist. 48
  In re Alien Children Education Litigation 50
  U.S. v. Texas 53
  Evans v. Buchanan 57

Idaho Migrant Council v. Board of Education 58
Castañeda v. Pickard 59
Heavy Runner v. Bremner 64
Keyes v. School District No. 1 Denver, Colorado 65
United States v. Board of Education of the
  City of Chicago 68
Gomez v. Illinois State Board of Education 71
Tangipahoa Parish School Board v. U.S. Department
  of Education 73
Teresa P. v. Berkeley Unified School District 75
People Who Care v. Rockford Board of Education ... 77
Ray M. v. Board of Education 81
OHA v. DOE 82
California Teachers Association v. Davis 85
Valeria v. Wilson 87

Chapter Four: Legislation and Statutes 91
  Fourteenth Amendment 91
  Title VI of the Civil Rights Act of 1964 91
  Equal Educational Opportunity Act of 1974 92
  Native American Language Act of 1990 93
  Individuals with Disabilities Education Act of 1997 .. 93
  Title III of the No Child Left Behind Act of 2001 ... 94

Chapter Five: Trends and Implications 101
  Fifth Circuit Court Cases 102
  Ninth Circuit Court Cases 103
  Other Circuit Court Cases 106
  Federal Statutes and Regulations 108
  No Child Left Behind Act 111

Resources 113

Index 115

About the Author 119

FOREWORD

The problems that language-minority students confront daily often are discussed, and recommendations for solving the problems of language-minority students are freely offered by both experts and laypersons. Federal and state statutes addressing issues related to language-minority students are enacted, regulations are adopted, and court decisions applying those statutes and regulations are handed down on a regular basis. But to understand the importance of educating language-minority students, one need not even visit our schools. Simply go to the places in your community where children and youth go, and the odds are excellent that you will encounter young people for whom English is not the first language and for whom English is quite a challenge.

Successfully educating all young people in our country, which must occur if we are to allow them the opportunity to participate fully in our society and economy, requires that we determine the best ways to educate the language-minority student, ways that are appropriate and permitted by law. Devoting limited education resources to achieve this end is much better than devoting those same limited resources to arguing, or even litigating, about what methods are either permitted or required. In this book Dr. Michael S. Mills sets out the legal framework that allows educators to devote their limited resources to educating students.

As a lawyer and legal educator, I must admit that I was skeptical that a layman would be able to analyze and interpret the many statutes and cases that address issues in the education of language-minority students. But Dr. Mills has done so very successfully and, in the process, taught me an important lesson. Each of us can learn from experts outside of our own discipline; each of us can expand our own understanding by learning what others are thinking. Through his careful analysis of relevant law, Dr. Mills has distilled many principles that education administrators and policy makers can use as a guide when deciding how to provide the best education to our students who are not proficient in the English language. His work will prove beneficial to all who work with language-minority students and thus will prove beneficial to our children and youth and ultimately to our country.

>Charles W. Goldner Jr., J.D., LL.M.
>Dean and Professor of Law
>William H. Bowen School of Law
>University of Arkansas at Little Rock

INTRODUCTION

According to a survey conducted by the Office of Educational Services for Limited English Proficient Children (formerly the Office of Bilingual Education and Minority Languages Affairs), limited-English proficient (LEP) student enrollment has increased at a dramatic rate in the United States. The OESLEPC projection showed a 104% increase in national LEP enrollments from 1989 to 1999. The survey indicated that this increase significantly outpaces the total K-12 enrollment increase of 13.6% (Macias 1998). The increasing number of language-minority students in U.S. schools is significant because the language barrier these children face is exacerbating the inequities of their education. Among persons between the ages of 16 and 24, 42% of those who reported difficulty with English had dropped out of high school, compared with only 10.5% of those who spoke only English (McArthur 1993). During the 1991-92 school year, 9% of the students classified as limited-English proficient were assigned to grade levels at least two years below age-grade norms (Fleischman and Hopstock 1993). Miramontes, Nadeau, and Commins added:

> Educating children from immigrant and ethnic minority group families is a major concern of school systems across the country. For many of these children, American education is not a successful experience. While one-tenth of non-Hispanic white students leave school without a diploma, one-fourth of African Americans, one-third of Hispanics, one-half of Native Americans, and two-thirds of all immigrant students drop out of school. (1997, p. ix)

The way to address this dismal situation is not clear. Although the plight of language-minority students has been a focus of concern for many decades, there is no certainty as to what an effective and meaningful education should be for LEP students (August and Hakuta 1997). Programs designed to address this issue vary considerably and range from total content instruction in the child's native language to total immersion in the English language. Determining which language policy provides the greatest benefit has been the focus of the bilingual education debate for decades. Schiffman (1996) characterizes language policy in the United States as lacking coherence and being composed of different components that act at cross-purposes. Furthermore, ambiguity in language education policy and law has sustained confusion and discrimination in school administration and education policy-making.

Cultural and linguistic diversity are challenging the premise that all students have a right to an equal education (Ovando and Collier 1985). Ovando and Collier state that students who are not fluent in English are labeled and defined by this characteristic, rather than by what they accomplish or the potential they possess.

From this conundrum came the advent of bilingual advocacy and its opposite, the English-only movement. Although both sides arm themselves with battalions of language scholars and evidence, both have failed in their attempts to present a sound education theory that supports children with limited or no English proficiency (Samway and McKeon 1999). This situation has yet to support the very children each side purports to help.

Thousands of children from virtually every cultural and linguistic background attend U.S. schools. According to August and Hakuta (1997), some districts deal with close to 125 languages spoken by students, among them Spanish, Vietnamese, Cantonese, Creole French, and Choctaw, to name just a few. And the upward trend in language-minority enrollment is staggering. According to an article in *Education Week*, the number of Latino students, a large proportion of whom are limited-English proficient, now outnumbers black students, making Latinos the largest minority group among schoolchildren younger than 18 years of age (Jacobson 1998).

According to Krashen (1999), school districts usually have done next to nothing to alleviate the academic strain that language-minority students struggle against. Many of these students come from low socioeconomic backgrounds and are doomed to failure. It is no surprise that many students from minority backgrounds drop out of school or otherwise fail to succeed (Krashen 1999). Left with ambiguous mandates from the federal government and politically charged initiatives from local governments, school districts have little direction and less vision for the future of this disadvantaged class of children (Samway and McKeon 1999).

Fradd and Tikunoff (1987) noted that education administrators are the persons primarily involved in determining school success and productivity, influencing not only the short-term goals of the institution but producing a vision of the long-term effect of schooling. Goodlad (1979) echoed this sentiment by stating that the roles of education administrators in influencing the lives of students must not be underestimated.

Language-minority students often are at high risk for academic failure. To combat this trend, schools and legislators need to understand how to provide these students with a meaningful education, to provide what Fradd and Tikunoff called "visionary leadership." This visionary leadership includes the ability to "develop effective programs, to model ways of valuing differences, and to organize schools into cohesive units that promote student achievement" (1987, p. 2). To do this, Fradd and Tikunoff indicate that:

> Administrators need to be well informed about the process of second language acquisition within the school context, and [administrators] need an understanding of terminology as well as the issues related to the education of students whose first language is not English. (1987, p. 2)

The purpose of this book is to help school administrators understand the legal principles involved in language policy and to apply those principles when making education policy and in everyday operational decisions. I have identified trends in legislation and case law within the context of language-minority education, including bilingual and English-only education, and related this information to principles that will guide school administrators and education policymakers. The cases are organized by decade and federal court district. The various principles were gleaned from federal litigation, statutes, and regulations related to language-minority education in the public schools.

The principles here are relevant and applicable to all language-minority situations in all states. Students throughout the United States are afforded the same basic rights under the Civil Rights Act of 1964 and the Equal Educational Opportunities Act of 1974. Exceptions to this general applicability are differences related to some form of English-only law in certain states. While every student has a right to remedial language assistance, even if he or she is the only language-minority student in the district, the student might not have access to a *bilingual* education.

The area of bilingual education is ever-changing. Recently California, Arizona, and Massachusetts adopted English-only education proposals, whereas Colorado rejected an English-only initiative. Notably, states that offer bilingual education services and those that restrict education to only English are continually shifting. For the latest information on which states accommodate bilingual education, one can contact the National Clearinghouse for English Language Acquisition (http://www.ncela.gwu.edu/states/index.htm).

Whatever the state, all students share the same basic civil rights and guarantee of equal educational opportunity. However, the various pedagogical approaches to achieve language proficiency are mired in controversy and politics. Regardless of any particular law or mandate to address the language-remediation needs of LEP children, a stark fact has continued to be unsettling. In 1986 the National Assessment of Educational Progress reported that fewer than 45% of language-minority Hispanic children were in programs specifically designed to overcome their language barriers (August and Garcia 1988). This reinforces the point that, though significant protections exist to remedy the language barriers of these language-minority children, there exists a gap in the placement of children in language remediation pro-

Introduction 5

grams. This problem seems to require a solution, a solution that can come only from education administrators and policymakers dedicated to meeting the needs of language-minority students in the United States.

Perhaps the most important guideline is simply understanding and using the parameters of educating language-minority students as the first step toward understanding which approaches best meet the needs of each student. The education administrator or policymaker holds responsibility for guiding language policy in his or her agency or district, and the responsibility will be best discharged if the administrator takes note of the guiding principles outlined above and further elaborated in the chapters that follow. This point was concisely made in *Cassell* v. *Texas* (1950):

> If one factor is uniform in a continuing series of events that are brought to pass through human intervention, the law would have to have the blindness of indifference rather than the blindness of impartiality not to attribute the uniform factor to man's purpose. The purpose may not be of evil intent or in conscious disregard of what is conceived to be a binding duty. Prohibited conduct may result from misconception of what duty requires. (p. 293)

Furthermore, assessing the language remediation program in each school district carries with it a tremendous responsibility, which is to ensure that equal educational opportunity exists. Administrators and policymakers are not urged to do this simply out of legal necessity; rather, they are urged to meet the needs of language-minority students out of moral necessity. Citing Bishop McCarthy's testimony from the *Federal Record*, the point of addressing the language needs of America's children becomes a luminous reality with a demanding charge:

> We are keeping certain people poor, and what we are manufacturing now is a monumental social cost to our society ten and fifteen and twenty years from now. . . . We are manufacturing ignorance; to be ignorant in society is to be nonproductive; to be nonproductive means for many

instances to be forced into a state of crime. . . . Whether it be right now in the form of modest increases in tuition, in public school operating cost, or . . . in terms of social cost . . . fifteen years from now, we will pay this bill. (Cong. Rec. Vol. VII, pp. 124-25)

CHAPTER ONE

A Ready Reference to Principles and Legal Requirements

Following is a ready reference to the general principles and legal requirements of educating language-minority students. I have compiled the 19 principles in this manner to provide a guide that busy education administrators and policymakers can use to navigate through the often ambiguous maze of language policies. Case or legislative citations follow the principles to indicate their bases.

1. Teachers and administrators do not have a right to use foreign languages in the classroom simply in the name of language rights (*Meyer* v. *Nebraska*).

2. State and local education agencies have an obligation to provide a language remediation program in any district where at least one language-minority student exists (EEOA, *Heavy Runner* v. *Bremner*).

3. Although states and local education agencies are required to implement language programs designed to overcome students' language barriers, school districts are not obligated to provide students with a bilingual-bicultural education in any foreign or Native American language. Moreover, school districts are not required to accommodate a group of language-minority children by establishing a language remediation program in a specific

school (NCLB, OCR guidelines, *Lau* v. *Nichols*, *Guadalupe* v. *Tempe*, *Otero* v. *Mesa*, *Deerfield* v. *Ipswich*, *OHA* v. *DOE*).

4. School districts and boards of education have the right to dictate what language remediation program will be implemented, as long as the program constitutes appropriate action under 20 U.S.C. §1703(f) (EEOA). To be appropriate, the program must meet three defining criteria: a) the school or agency is pursuing a program that is based on sound pedagogical theory or legitimate experimental strategy, b) the program or strategy is reasonably calculated to implement effective education theory by the school or agency, and c) the program produces results indicating that language barriers are actually being overcome (*Castañeda* v. *Pickard*, OCR guidelines).

5. The goal of any language remediation program must be transitional in nature; that is, its purpose must be to integrate and encourage contact between English-speaking and language-minority children as soon as possible (OCR guidelines, NCLB, *U.S.* v. *Texas*).

6. Not only do local education agencies have a responsibility to implement a language remediation program designed to overcome language barriers, state education agencies have a responsibility to directly monitor district compliance with respect to any language remediation program (OCR guidelines, NCLB, *Gomez* v. *Illinois Board of Education*).

7. Education agencies are required not only to overcome the direct obstacle of a language barrier, but also to provide students with assistance in other curricular areas in which equal participation is limited because of participation in a language remediation program (OCR guidelines, NCLB, *Lau* v. *Nichols*, *People Who Care* v. *Rockford*).

8. Schools are required to serve the needs of all of their language-minority students, including illegal, undocumented aliens (*Plyler* v. *Doe*, *In re Alien Children Litigation*).

9. Failure to provide more than what is minimally required in a language remediation program does not qualify as a discriminatory course of conduct condemned by the Equal Protection Clause (*Guadalupe* v. *Tempe*, *San Antonio* v. *Rodriguez*).

10. School districts may be required by a court to mandate steps to help teachers recognize the home language of their minority students, whether it be a foreign language or simply a cultural dialect of English (*Martin Luther King Jr. Elementary School Children* v. *Ann Arbor School District*).

11. To prove a violation of §601 of the Civil Rights Act or the Equal Protection Clause of the Fourteenth Amendment, one is required to show that intentional discrimination is caused by a district's language policy or present actions. However, if the purpose of the litigation is simply to enforce the regulations of the Civil Rights Act through injunctive effort, one is required only to show that discriminatory effect exists (*Lau* v. *Nichols*, *Washington* v. *Davis*, *Valeria* v. *Wilson*).

12. If a school district is making a good-faith effort to provide equal educational opportunity, it is unnecessary for teachers or tutors to hold language-specific credentials in order to deliver remediation programs to language-minority students (*Teresa* v. *Berkeley Unified School District*). However, a district that accepts funds through Title III of the No Child Left Behind Act must ensure that its teachers are qualified to teach in the language remediation program and, if teaching a bilingual education program, are fluent in the languages being taught (NCLB).

13. Federal law requires language-remediation and IDEA placement testing, and all pursuant notifications must be done in the student's native language. All such testing must be free of racial or cultural bias (IDEA).

14. Within the context of a desegregation case, failure to take appropriate action under §1703(f) violates any desegregation mandate (*People Who Care* v. *Rockford Board*, *Keyes* v. *Denver School District No. 1*).

15. Desegregation remedies, whether through transportation or placement policies, cannot stigmatize, burden, or deprive equal educational opportunity to a third ethnic class, particularly language-minority students (*People Who Care* v. *Rockford Board*, *Keyes* v. *Denver School District No. 1*).

16. Federal courts may consider the actions of a district with respect to its language remediation program to evaluate the entire school system in a desegregation case (*People Who Care* v. *Rockford Board*, *Keyes* v. *Denver School District No. 1*).

17. Districts and state education agencies cannot admit or exclude students from any federally assisted education program, notably Title III, on the basis of a surname or language-minority status (OCR guidelines, NCLB).

18. Care must be taken when accepting funds authorized through Title III of the No Child Left Behind Act, for acceptance of funds places a contractual agreement on the education agency to abide by the more stringent guidelines of the law, especially with respect to the number of years students can learn in their native language and the attendant testing and parental notification requirements (NCLB).

19. Schools should consider abiding by the guidelines set forth by the Office of Civil Rights, for they represent the most widely accepted interpretation of language-minority education rights (*Castañeda* v. *Pickard*, OCR guidelines).

OCR Compliance Reviews

Although many people believe that litigation against a school district is the only method to ensure that language remediation laws and statutes are enforced, the most common enforcement method is initiated by the Office of Civil Rights (OCR). Since many, if not most, school districts accept some type of federal funding, the more stringent civil rights guidelines established in 1964 apply.

Such reviews are designed to determine whether schools are complying with their obligations under Title VI of the Civil Rights Act of 1964 to provide language remediation programs necessary to ensure that LEP students have meaningful access to the schools' education programs. OCR compliance requirements for Title VI are the same as the requirements the federal courts have established for compliance with the Equal Educational Opportunity statute.

The OCR guidelines are compiled from the various OCR memos. These include the 27 September 1991 memo, titled "Policy Update on Schools' Obligations Toward National Origin Minority Students with Limited-English Proficiency (LEP students)"; the 3 December 1985 memo, titled "The Office for Civil Rights' Title VI Language Minority Compliance Procedures"; and the May 1970 memo to school districts, titled "Identification of Discrimination and Denial of Services on the Basis of National origin," 35 Fed. Reg. 11595 (also known as the May Memorandum).

The Office of Civil Rights examines two areas in determining whether a school is in compliance with Title VI: 1) the need for a language remediation program for LEP students, and 2) the adequacy of the program chosen by the school to allow LEP students to participate more effectively in the school's educational program. Within these two broad areas are specific concerns, such as segregation of LEP students, program staffing requirements, exit criteria, and placement of LEP students in exceptional education programs.

Need for a Program

School districts must have procedures in place for identifying and assessing LEP students. According to the OCR, the type of program that is necessary to adequately identify students in need of services will vary widely, depending on the demographics of the particular school. Even in districts with few LEP students, teachers and administrators should be informed of their obligations to provide alternative language services to students in need of such services and of their obligation to seek any assistance necessary to comply with this requirement. Schools with a significant LEP population are expected to have a more formal program.

Under rare circumstances a school district may not be required to have a language remediation program for its LEP students. For example, if a school district contends that its LEP students have equal and significant access to the district's programs despite the lack of a language remediation program, the school district will have to prove that its LEP students are performing as well as their non-LEP peers in the district with respect to achievement and retention rates.

Segregation of LEP Students. Providing special services to LEP students may segregate LEP students during the school day, but case law states that this segregation is permissible because "the benefits which would accrue to [LEP] students by remedying the language barriers which impede their ability to realize their academic potential in an English language educational institution may outweigh the adverse effects of such segregation" (*Castañeda*, 648 F. 2d at 998).

The focus of the OCR will be on whether the district's language remediation program — whether it is ESL, transitional bilingual education, developmental bilingual education, bilingual/bicultural education, or structured immersion — provides the least segregation possible.

According to the Office of Civil Rights 1991 Policy Update Memo, specific practices that violate the antisegregation provisions of Title VI include "segregating LEP students for both academic and nonacademic subjects, such as recess, physical education, art and music and keeping students in language remediation program longer than necessary to ensure equal educational opportunity for the student."

Placement in Exceptional Education Programs. OCR policy, according to the May Memorandum of 1970, is that school systems may not assign students to special education programs on assessments that measure and evaluate English language skills. The additional legal requirements imposed by Section 504 also must be considered when conducting investigations on this issue.

Through policy memos, the OCR has determined that *Lau* compliance reviews will include inquiries into the placement of LEP students in special education programs if there are indications that LEP students may be inappropriately placed in such programs or when special education programs provided for LEP students do not address their inability to speak or understand English.

Exclusion of LEP students from gifted and talented programs may violate the provisions of Title VI, unless the exclusion is justified by the needs of the particular student or by the nature of the specialized program. However, according to the OCR in its 1991 memo:

> LEP students cannot be categorically excluded from gifted or talented or other specialized programs. If a recipient has a process for locating and identifying gifted or talented students, it must also locate and identify gifted or talented LEP students who could benefit from the program.

School districts must explain any lack of participation by LEP students to the students, their parents, and the Office of Civil Rights. The only justifications for excluding a particular LEP student from a program include:

> (1) that time for the program would unduly hinder his or her participation in an alternative language program, and (2) that the specialized program itself requires proficiency in English language skills for meaningful participation.

Thus school districts must take precautions to ensure that evaluation and testing procedures do not screen out LEP students because of their limited-English proficiency.

Program Adequacy

Title VI fulfillment of an adequate program is determined by the OCR if the following conditions, which stem from the *Castañeda* decision, are met (although EEOA is not enforced by the OCR, the *Castañeda* principles emanate from the EEOA statute). It is important to note that the Office of Civil Rights does not mandate any particular program of instruction for LEP students.

Acceptable conditions of a language remediation program include:

1. The program the recipient chooses is recognized as sound by some experts in the field or is considered a legitimate experimental strategy.

2. The programs and practices used by the school system are reasonably calculated to implement effectively the education theory adopted by the school.

3. The program succeeds, after a legitimate trial, in producing results indicating that students' language barriers are actually being overcome.

The three-pronged *Castañeda* standard is the OCR-approved method for determining the adequacy of a school's efforts to provide equal education opportunities for LEP students. The real keys are the soundness of the approach to educating LEP students and ensuring its proper implementation. In terms of soundness, *Castañeda* requires districts to use education theories that are recognized as sound by some experts in the field, or at least theories that are recognized as legitimate education strategies. Some approaches that fall under this category include transitional bilingual education, bilingual/bicultural education, structured immersion, developmental bilingual education, and English as a second language. The OCR evaluates the proper implementation of a language remediation program with respect to: staffing requirements for programs, exit criteria, and access to exceptional education programs, such as gifted and talented programs.

Staffing Requirements. School districts must hire formally qualified teachers for LEP students or require that teachers obtain formal qualifications. Essentially, if the school district requires teachers of non-LEP students to be certified in their content areas, then teachers of LEP students also must be certified in the same manner. This requirement is reaffirmed in the recent Title III legislation.

School districts implementing a bilingual program for LEP students must require that bilingual education teachers be fluent in all of the languages they teach. Teachers also must have received adequate instruction in bilingual education methods. School districts that use methods other than bilingual education — for example, ESL or structured immersion programs — must ensure that teachers in their programs also have been adequately trained, whether through inservice training or formal college coursework in the methods used. A commensurate level of training applies to bilingual aides, but school administrators and teachers must take care not to relegate actual instruction to aides.

School districts that have tried unsuccessfully to hire qualified teachers must provide adequate training to teachers already on staff as soon as possible. However, it must be noted that school districts must require non-credentialed employees to be trained immediately so that they can teach effectively and function adequately, even as they are working toward their certification.

Program Evaluation. Castañeda requires school districts to modify their programs if they prove to be unsuccessful after a legitimate trial. This means the school district must conduct periodic evaluations of its language remediation program and modify the program if it does not meet the needs of its LEP students.

Exit Criteria for LEP Students. Students may not be placed in a language remediation program indefinitely. They should be provided with services only until they are proficient in English to an extent that will allow them to participate meaningfully in the regular education program. "Exit criteria" are used to determine when LEP students may or must move from language remediation to regular education.

The OCR has established factors that determine whether LEP students are able to participate meaningfully in regular education:

- They are able to keep up with their non-LEP peers in the regular education program.
- They are able to participate successfully in all aspects of the school's curriculum without the use of simplified English materials.
- Their retention-in-grade and dropout rates are similar to those of their non-LEP peers.

The exit criteria that school districts establish must be based on objective measurements, such as standardized test scores, and must include assessment of the student's oral language proficiency. The district should be able to show how students meeting the exit criteria will be able to participate meaningfully in the regular classroom.

Schools that design their LEP programs to emphasize English over other subjects for a period of time may discontinue special instruction in English once LEP students become English-proficient. However, such schools still must provide remedial assistance as necessary to address academic deficits that may have occurred while the student was learning English.

CHAPTER TWO

A Recent History of Language Policy in the United States

According to Crawford (1995), the United States has always been at odds with itself, condemning foreign languages and promoting English during periods of external strife and nationalistic fervor. In fact, many U.S. citizens in the 18th century were bilingual, just as many in the 21st century still speak a language other than English. Yet today, Americanization efforts have extended to making English the exclusive, official language of the United States (Piatt 1990) — even though the nation is faced with an ever-growing language-minority population (Crawford 1995; Piatt 1990; Anstrom 1996). The effect of this conflict is an incoherent and ambiguous language policy, composed of different components that act at cross-purposes to one another. This confusion extends to the ambiguity in education policymaking regarding language-minority populations (Schiffman 1996).

Bilingual education enjoyed a surge in the 19th century, though various groups toward the end of that century sought to diminish bilingual education rights. According to Crawford (1995), the manifestation of this trend can be seen in the decline in German-language schooling, which was abandoned by an increasing number of school districts. St. Louis is one such school district that Crawford described as abandoning bilingual education after its German voting strength was weakened by the advent of World War I.

The first half of the 20th century witnessed considerable intolerance toward foreigners. This prevailing mood in U.S. society was exemplified by the laws of several states that displayed a hostile attitude toward foreigners and foreign languages (Goldstein, Gee, and Daniel 1995). Such intolerance continues today (Soto 1997), as exemplified by the fact that language rights exist in the United States only as a component of other rights, in particular the Equal Protection Clause of the Fourteenth Amendment, Title VI of the Civil Rights Act of 1964 (42 U.S.C. §2000(d)), and the Equal Educational Opportunity Act of 1974 (20 U.S.C. §1703(f)).

The Supreme Court (*Meyer* v. *State of Nebraska*, 1923) struck down restrictions on foreign language instruction as unconstitutional, a violation of due process guarantees. In this case an instructor in a Zionist parochial school was tried and convicted in Nebraska for unlawfully teaching the subject of reading using a German Bible history book. The challenged law forbade the teaching of any subject in a language other than English. It also forbade the teaching of any other language, with the exception of so-called dead languages, until the pupil had attained and successfully passed the eighth grade. The Supreme Court held this particular state law to be unconstitutional. The basis rested on the Fourteenth Amendment guarantee to protect individuals from arbitrary or unreasonable state action impairing life, liberty, or property interests. The Fourteenth Amendment to the United States Constitution states:

> No State shall make or enforce any law which shall abridge the privileges or immunities of citizens of the United States, nor shall any state deprive any person of life, liberty, or property, without due process of law; nor deny to any person within its jurisdiction the equal protection of the laws.

This constitutional mandate has become a cornerstone in the protection of civil rights and equal educational opportunity for public school students.

Bilingual education surged in the 1960s with the influx of Cubans into Miami after the 1959 Cuban revolution. In 1961 the Dade County Public School District provided English-as-a-second-language (ESL) instruction and later established a full bilingual education program at Coral Way Elementary School (Stein 1986).

To ensure equal protection under the Fourteenth Amendment, bilingual education funding for local school districts was authorized by Title VII of the Bilingual Education Act of 1968, a new provision of the Elementary and Secondary Education Act of 1964. This provision funded 76 bilingual programs in its first year (Blanco 1978). Congress passed this legislation to support the growing number of immigrant children who, because of their limited English proficiency, were not receiving an education equal to their English-proficient peers. Title VII continues to fund bilingual programs through ESEA, which was reauthorized through the Improving America's Schools Act of 1994 (IASA) and the No Child Left Behind Act of 2001 (NCLB).

Established by Congress in 1974, the Office of Bilingual Education and Minority Language Affairs was created to help school districts meet this responsibility to provide equal educational opportunity to limited-English-proficient children (Crawford 1995). Impetus for the creation of this office came, in part, from the Supreme Court decision in *Lau* v. *Nichols* (1974). This landmark bilingual education case was a class-action lawsuit by Chinese-speaking students against the San Francisco Unified School District. Of the approximately 2,900 students of Chinese ancestry who did not speak English in that school district, 1,800 students were not given supplemental English instruction. The plaintiffs in the case alleged that the district violated the Equal Protection Clause of the Fourteenth Amendment and Title VI of the Civil Rights Act of 1964 by not providing them with remedial English instruction.

The Civil Rights Act of 1964 has been a significant part of the language policy issue, banning all forms of discrimination on the grounds of race, color, or national origin in any federally funded program. The statute states, in part:

> No person in the United States shall, on the ground of race, color, or national origin, be excluded from participa-

tion in, be denied the benefits of, or be subjected to discrimination under any program or activity receiving Federal financial assistance. (42 U.S.C. §2000(d))

The accompanying regulation, specific to the Department of Education, echoes the wording of 42 U.S.C. §2000(d) and prohibits discrimination in education programs:

> No person in the United States shall, on the ground of race, color, or national origin be excluded from participation in, be denied the benefits of, or be otherwise subjected to discrimination under any program to which this part applies. (34 C.F.R. §100.3)

The Supreme Court decided that the San Francisco schools had the responsibility to instruct students in English. The Court pointed out an applicable regulation that had been promulgated by the predecessor to the current Department of Education, the U.S. Department of Health, Education and Welfare. The requirement stated:

> Where inability to speak and understand the English language excludes national-origin minority group children from effectively participating in the educational program offered by a school district, the district must take affirmative steps to rectify the language deficiency in order to open its instructional program to these students. (35 Fed. Reg. 11595)

This regulation, better known as the May 1970 Memorandum, was a clarification of earlier guidelines related to the Civil Rights Act of 1964. Basing their decision in part on this regulation, the Supreme Court stated that there is no equality of treatment merely by providing students with the same facilities, textbooks, teachers, and curriculum. Rather, students who do not understand English are inhibited from receiving any meaningful education. Thus the Court ordered that school districts with such students must take affirmative action to overcome language barriers.

In 1975, following the decision in *Lau*, the Education Commissioner of the Department of Health, Education and Welfare formulated guidelines for school district compliance with Title VI of the Civil Rights Act of 1964. This issue was prominent because the *Lau* decision set forth several requirements for meeting the civil rights obligations under Title VI. Those guidelines, presented under the title, "Task Force Findings Specifying Remedies Available for Eliminating Past Educational Practices Ruled Unlawful Under *Lau* v. *Nichols*," were distributed as a memorandum to school districts but were never published in the Federal Register. These guidelines later were called the "Lau Remedies" or "Lau Guidelines," specific procedures for identifying and evaluating language-minority students' English skills, determining appropriate instructional strategies and transition strategies to mainstream English classrooms, and determining the professional standards to be met by teachers of language-minority children.

The Lau Guidelines required bilingual instruction, obligating school districts not employing bilingual education programs to demonstrate that their programs were as effective as the bilingual programs described in the guidelines. The Lau Guidelines met considerable resistance even though they had become, though unofficially, the legal standard that the Office of Civil Rights used to determine an education agency's compliance with Title VI. By 1980 the OCR had conducted more than 600 compliance reviews, leading to the negotiation of 359 school district *Lau* plans (Crawford 1995). However, several school districts resisted the *Lau* plans and openly balked at their adoption. The resistance eventually turned to complaints of intrusiveness on the part of the federal government. A group of Alaska school districts challenged the legality of the Lau Remedies and won, in settlement, a promise by the government to formally approve rules on school district compliance with Title VI (*Northwest Arctic* v. *Califano*, 1978). The new regulations, proposed by President Carter in 1980, promptly were withdrawn in 1981 in the early days of President Reagan's administration (Crawford 1995).

The courts moved away from determinations of district compliance to Title VI. Instead, many courts began to rely on the Equal Educational Opportunity Act of 1974, which requires appropriate action by a school district in overcoming language barriers that impede a student's equal participation in the education process. The law states:

> No State shall deny equal educational opportunity to an individual on account of his or her race, color, sex, or national origin, by the failure by an educational agency to take appropriate action to overcome language barriers that impede equal participation by its students in its instructional programs. (20 U.S.C. §1703(f))

This statute has become a standard for establishing language remediation programs in the United States, particularly with the decision in *Castañeda* v. *Pickard* (1981), which established specific criteria for determining if a language remediation program constituted what the statute calls "appropriate action." The OCR, the primary enforcer of language-minority rights under Title VI, actively uses the *Castañeda* guidelines, thus ensuring "appropriate action" under the EEOA requirements.

Now more than ever, language diversity is commanding the attention of educators. In the past several decades this diversity has increased substantially, as measured by the variety of languages spoken in the United States by minority-language speakers and, most dramatically, by the enrollment of LEP students. The 1990 census counted 6.3 million youths, ages 5 to 17, who spoke a language other than English at home. According to Anstrom (1996), this was a 38% increase over the previous decade, a period in which the overall school-age population declined by 4.5%. By a more expansive definition of language-minority, that is, living in a home where a non-English language is spoken, there were 9.9 million language-minority children, 22% of the school-age population (Anstrom 1996). More than 325 languages are now used at home by U.S. residents, including at least 137 Native American languages, according to the Census Bureau (1993). The growth of this linguistically diverse population is especially rapid in a handful of states, six of which enroll an estimated 72% of the nation's LEP students (U.S. General Accounting Office 1994).

Faced with this increasing language-minority population, many activist groups have lobbied for provisions to protect the English language. Stein (1986) compiled a record of the numerous legislative efforts in the early 1980s to make English the official language of the United States. Although nothing has come of a federal statute or constitutional amendment that would codify English as America's official language, many states have passed measures making English the official language of that state (Piatt 1990). Twenty-one states have enforced official-English laws in statute or in their constitutions, including Arkansas, California, Colorado, Florida, Georgia, Illinois, Indiana, Kentucky, Louisiana, Mississippi, Missouri, Montana, Nebraska, New Hampshire, North Carolina, North Dakota, South Carolina, South Dakota, Tennessee, Virginia, and Wyoming.

According to Piatt (1990), the conventional wisdom of English-only advocates is that a federal constitutional amendment would be passed easily if a majority of states would adopt the official English language position. During the past several sessions of Congress, a resolution that proposes an amendment to the Constitution to make English the official language of the United States has been introduced. Many other bills also have been introduced with the same expressed purpose of making English the nation's official language. Crawford (1995) explains a few of the ramifications of such programs in clear terms: the elimination of bilingual 911 operators, health-care workers, and teachers.

On the other hand, the influence of the English-only movement has spurred a backlash in the form of English Plus, a campaign intent on teaching LEP students English while preserving their native languages for the sake of ethnic pride. The English Plus coalition, according to Piatt (1990), has endeavored to educate the public about the necessity of respecting language rights. Piatt also mentions that many legislators, such as John Breaux of Louisiana and Daniel Inouye of Hawaii, have taken up this cause in an effort to protect the language rights of their constituents. Furthermore, the federal courts have stepped up their focus on language rights and have begun to be clearer in identifying the basis for the need to protect language rights (Piatt 1990).

This infighting between pro-English and pro-bilingual forces is evident in the contentious changes sweeping the federal bilingual education program. The federal courts have been active in recent decades, establishing key decisions and interpreting federal laws to define more clearly each state's obligation to language-minority children. In particular, federal case law related to language policy has begun to focus on three major statutory issues: the Civil Rights Act of 1964, the Equal Educational Opportunities Act, and the Equal Protection Clause of the Fourteenth Amendment. In addition, many laws, both sweeping and token, have been passed, including many reauthorizations to the Bilingual Education Act, now known as Title III of the No Child Left Behind Act (NCLB), and the Native American Language Act of 1992.

CHAPTER THREE

A Compendium of Court Decisions

This compendium begins with court decisions, which are arranged chronologically. The next chapter summarizes legislation and statutes.

Meyer v. State of Nebraska, 262 U.S. 390 (1923)

Facts and Issues. An instructor in a Zionist parochial school was tried and convicted in Nebraska for unlawfully teaching the subject of reading in the German language. The challenged law forbade the teaching in school of any subject in a language other than English and also forbade the teaching of any other language, with the exception of so-called dead languages, until the pupil had attained and successfully passed the eighth grade.

Holding. The Supreme Court held that the state law forbidding the teaching of foreign languages is unconstitutional.

Reasoning. The Court's basis rested on the Fourteenth Amendment guarantee to protect individuals from arbitrary or unreasonable state action impairing life, liberty, or property interests. Furthermore, the right to teach is protected by the Fourteenth Amendment. The purpose of the Nebraska law, according to the Supreme Court:

was to promote civic development by inhibiting training and education of the immature in foreign tongues and ideals before they could learn English and acquire American ideals, and that the "English language should be and become the mother tongue of all children reared in this state." (p. 401)

The Court decided that, because there is no clear danger to the state that stems from younger children studying foreign languages, the reason given for the teacher's conviction was unreasonable and arbitrary:

> While this court has not attempted to define with exactness the liberty thus guaranteed . . . without doubt, it denotes not merely freedom from bodily restraint but also the right of an individual to . . . enjoy privileges long recognized at common law as essential to the orderly pursuit of happiness by free men. The established doctrine is that this liberty may not be interfered with, under the guise of protecting the public interest, by legislative action which is arbitrary or without reasonable relation to some purpose within the competency of the state to effect. (p. 399)

Significance of Ruling. The Court's decision was the first ruling to protect the rights of teachers who taught in a foreign language. This further expanded teachers' academic freedom rights. Significantly, the Court did not rule in favor of promoting the teaching of a second language; rather, it ruled in favor of the teacher's right simply to teach. That is, teachers do not have the right to teach in the name of language rights, only in the right of academic freedom. In no way were bilingual language rights guaranteed:

> The power of the state to compel attendance at some school and to make reasonable regulations for all schools, including a requirement that they shall give instructions in English, is not questioned. Nor has challenge been made of the state's power to prescribe a curriculum for institutions which it supports. . . . No emergency has arisen which renders knowledge by a child of some language other than English so clearly harmful as to justify its inhibition with the consequent infringement of rights long freely enjoyed. (p. 402)

The implicit meaning of this decision is understood more clearly with Justice Oliver Wendell Holmes' dissent, stating that all U.S. citizens should be required to speak a common tongue. Notably, the Court did not counter his position. In this manner, the Court affirmed the right of the state to establish English-only policies and rejected the primacy of language rights for individuals.

Bartels v. Iowa, 262 U.S. 404 (1923)

Facts and Issues. Several parochial school teachers in Iowa and Ohio were convicted of violating state statutes prohibiting them from teaching foreign languages to students who had not yet completed the eighth grade. This case combined the various appeals.

Holding. The Court held that any state law forbidding the teaching of a foreign language to any student is unconstitutional. The Supreme Court reversed the lower courts' rulings.

Reasoning. The Court based its decision on the previous decision in *Meyer* v. *Nebraska* (1923) — the laws limiting the teaching of modern foreign languages violate the Fourteenth Amendment guarantee of liberty interests for teachers and students.

Significance of Ruling. This ruling reaffirmed the decision in the *Meyer* case of the same year. Notably, the Court added a significant opinion to *Meyer*. Justices Holmes and Sutherland dissented and warned that the ruling sent the wrong message to America regarding the teaching of foreign languages. Justice Holmes indicated that the respective statutes prohibiting the teaching of foreign languages were reasonable means of maintaining English as the only spoken language in the United States. Holmes stated:

> We all agree, I take it, that it is desirable that all the citizens of the United States should speak a common tongue, and therefore that the end aimed at by the statute is a lawful and proper one. . . . Youth is the time when familiarity with a language is established and if there are sections in the State

> where a child would hear only Polish or German spoken at home, I am not prepared to say that it is unreasonable to provide that in his early years he shall hear and speak only English at school. (p. 412)

Justice Holmes passionately indicated that the Court supported, at least in some measure, the idea that English-only instruction was desirable, if not essential, for the United States.

Arvizu v. *Waco Independent School District,* 373 F. Supp. 1264 (W.D. Tex. 1973)

Facts and Issues. This case was a combined desegregation suit that black and Mexican-American students and parents filed against the Waco school district. Acknowledging difficulty in determining whether Mexican Americans had truly been the victims of discrimination, the court relied on the Fourteenth Amendment, which prohibits segregation in public schools resulting from state action. The court stated that the Fifth Circuit precedent set in *Cisneros* v. *CCISD* (1972) was that a finding of unlawful segregation rested on the proof of a denial of equal educational opportunity manifested through racial or ethnic segregation as a result of state action.

Holding. The court rejected any finding of state-imposed segregation of Mexican-American students.

Reasoning. The court found that the state and the school district were not responsible for the disproportionate placement of its Mexican-American students, which was the result of residential housing patterns. The court also noted the plaintiffs' failure to prove that the district or state officially and intentionally tried to segregate Mexican-American students from other races.

However, relying on the *Cisneros* v. *CCISD* decision, the court found that the Mexican-American students constituted "an identifiable ethnic minority, recognizable by their numbers, concentration, cultural uniqueness, and common special needs and problems" (p. 1269).

The court continued by linking certain privileges and rights to the Mexican-American children because of their status as an identifiable ethnic class with educational needs. Two such entitlements were "protection against being classified as 'whites' for purposes of desegregating racially identifiable black schools," and the "implementation of a curriculum and special educational programs, such as bilingual education, necessary to provide equal educational opportunities for Mexican-American students as a group" (p. 1269).

Significance of Ruling. This case, though coming before *Lau*, was a significant decision affirming the right of Mexican-American children to equal educational opportunities through a language remediation program. The case is also noteworthy in that it highlights a future debate pitting the value of desegregation efforts against the value of bilingual education programs. This case stated that a disproportionate number of Mexican-American students in one school was acceptable, and even desired, so as to "combat the lowering of self-image concept." (p.1280).

Lau v. Nichols, 414 U.S. 563 (1974)

Facts and Issues. This landmark bilingual education case was a class-action lawsuit by Chinese-speaking students against the San Francisco Unified School District. Of the approximately 2,900 students of Chinese ancestry who did not speak English in that school district, 1,800 students were not given supplemental English instruction. According to California statute, the policy of the state was to ensure English mastery by all students. California law also required all students to be proficient in English in order to graduate and to receive a high school diploma. The plaintiffs in the case alleged the school district violated the Equal Protection Clause of the Fourteenth Amendment and Title VI of the Civil Rights Act of 1964 by not providing them with remedial English instruction.

Holding. In a unanimous decision, the Supreme Court reversed the decision of the Court of Appeals and decided that the responsibility to instruct students in English rested with the San Francisco schools.

Reasoning. Although the Supreme Court did not view the violation of the Equal Protection Clause as substantive, it did rule in favor of the students based on §601 of the Civil Rights Act of 1964. That section bans discrimination based "on the ground of race, color, or national origin" in "any program or activity receiving federal financial assistance" (42 U.S.C. §2000(d)). According to federal regulations related to §601, discrimination is barred if it has the effect of "defeating or substantially impairing accomplishment of the objectives of the program as respect individuals of a particular race, color, or national origin" (45 C.F.R. §80.3(b)(2)). Noting that the San Francisco schools received a substantial amount of federal financial assistance, the Court opined that "the Chinese-speaking minority receives fewer benefits than the English-speaking majority from respondents' school system which denies them a meaningful opportunity to participate in the educational program" (p. 568).

Although no intent by the district to discriminate was present, the effect of its policy was discriminatory according to federal law. The Court further alluded to an applicable requirement by the then U.S. Department of Health, Education and Welfare. The guideline, known as the May 1970 Memorandum, an unofficial rule, stated:

> Where inability to speak and understand the English language excludes national-origin minority group children from effectively participating in the educational program offered by a school district, the district must take affirmative steps to rectify the language deficiency in order to open its instructional program to these students. (33 Fed. Reg. 11595)

The Court indicated that there is no equality of treatment merely by providing students with the same facilities, textbooks, teachers, and curriculum. Rather, students who do not understand English are inhibited from receiving any meaningful education.

Significance of Ruling. Following the decision in *Lau*, HEW developed what were later called the "Lau Guidelines," which offered a suggested compliance plan for school districts. The Educational Opportunities Act of 1974 echoed HEW's May 1970 Memorandum by requiring affirmative action by a school district in overcoming language barriers that impede a student's equal participation in the educational process. This law, 20 U.S.C. §1703 et seq., has become a defining aspect of later language-policy litigation. Notably, Justice Blackmun's concurring opinion in this decision was conditional. He stated that remedial measures would be necessary only if many children were being disadvantaged:

> Against the possibility that the Court's judgment may be interpreted too broadly, I stress the fact that the children with whom we are concerned here number about 1,800. This is a very substantial group that is being deprived of any meaningful schooling because the children cannot understand the language of the classroom. We may only guess as to why they have had no exposure to English in their preschool years. Earlier generations of American ethnic groups have overcome the language barrier by earnest parental endeavor or by the hard fact of being pushed out of the family or community nest and into the realities of broader experience. I merely wish to make plain that when, in another case, we are concerned with a very few youngsters, or with just a single child who speaks only German or Polish or Spanish or any language other than English, I would not regard today's decision, or the separate concurrence, as conclusive upon the issue whether the statute and the guideline require the funded school district to provide special instruction. For me, *numbers are the heart of this case* and my concurrence is to be understood accordingly. (p. 572, emphasis added)

Serna v. *Portales*, 499 F.2d 1147 (10th Cir. 1974)

Facts and Issues. The plaintiffs in this case alleged that there was discrimination in the Portales School District in that it failed to provide bilingual instruction that takes into account the special education needs of its Mexican-American students, failed to hire any teachers or administrators of Mexican-American descent, and failed to structure a curriculum that took into account the educational and cultural needs of Mexican-American children. Serna alleged that this discrimination violated the Fourteenth Amendment right of equal protection and protection from discrimination guaranteed by 42 U.S.C. §2000(d), specifically known as §601 of the Civil Rights Act.

Holding. The court held that the Portales School District violated §601 of the Civil Rights Act with respect to the education of its language-minority students by not providing the plaintiffs with a bilingual-bicultural education program. The court failed to decide on the Equal Protection issue because of the recent decision in *Lau*.

Reasoning. The court ruled in favor of Serna, the representative of Latino children, against whom the district had discriminated. The court stated:

> The factual situation in the instant case is strikingly similar to that found in *Lau*. Appellees are Spanish surnamed students who prior to this lawsuit were placed in totally English speaking schools. There is substantial evidence that most of these Spanish surnamed students are deficient in the English language; nevertheless no affirmative steps were taken by the Portales school district to rectify these language deficiencies. (p.1153)

Relying on the *Lau* decision by the Supreme Court, the district court further noted that the Portales School District's failure to provide the Latino children with any program of instruction designed for their needs was in direct violation of the 1964 Civil Rights Act.

Significance of Ruling. This lower-court decision reaffirmed the actions taken by the Supreme Court in *Lau*. More significantly, the court said it could order a bilingual-bicultural education program and the hiring of more Spanish-speaking teachers in order to foster equal educational opportunity for all students.

The court also countered the New Mexico State Board of Education's concern that radical means would have to be taken wherever a language-minority student was found. The court also noted Supreme Court Justice Blackmun's argument, which was that the number of disadvantaged students is the focal concern of any complaint and that only when a substantial group is being deprived of a meaningful education will a Title VI violation exist.

Morales v. *Turman*, 383 F. Supp. 53 (E.D. Tex. 1974)

Facts and Issues. The plaintiffs in this case were juveniles classified as delinquent who were committed involuntarily to the Texas Youth Council (TYC) juvenile detention centers for various crimes. The TYC comprised six training schools, three for females and three for males. This case began as an injunction sought by two attorneys who were attempting to communicate privately with their clients and send and receive uncensored mail. The litigation grew to include numerous complaints against the TYC system, including the issue of bilingual education.

Even though a significant number of inmates at TYC training centers were Spanish-speaking Mexican Americans, no bilingual programs existed in any of the TYC institutions. Furthermore, intelligence and reading achievement tests were not conducted in Spanish for language-minority students. The court called this a significant deficiency because decisions regarding placement of students in education programs at Gatesville were made primarily on the basis of the test scores. All inmates at Gatesville who could not read English were placed in the same remedial reading class. Thus Spanish-speaking students, mentally retarded children, and those who were unable to read because of emotional reasons or past truancy were placed in the same class. In addition, the tests for Spanish-speaking boys who may have had learning disabilities, such as dyslexia, were not given in Spanish.

Holding. The court held, among other things, that the state had an obligation to provide bilingual education to Mexican-American juveniles in the TYC system. The court also mandated the use of culturally neutral psychological, intelligence, and reading achievement tests.

Reasoning. The court reasoned that, because the state removes Mexican-American children "from their family, friends, ethnic background and culture, transporting them in most cases hundreds of miles to a predominantly Anglo rural setting" (p. 90), the state has an obligation to establish a program for bilingual education. The justification for this remedy was based on the testimony of experts in education. In this case, the program had to be set up according to the guidelines set forth in *United States* v. *Texas* (1972).

Significance of Ruling. This case, coming at the same time as the Supreme Court's decision in *Lau*, explicitly required a state education institution to provide bilingual education to Mexican-American children who were classified as language-minority students. However, the decision lacked any federal or state statutory basis. The court's mandates were based on the testimony of expert witnesses. Significantly, in the following year the Education for All Handicapped Children's Act, later amended and renamed the Individuals with Disabilities Education Act, would require placement testing in a child's native language (20 U.S.C. §1415 et. seq.).

Otero v. *Mesa,* 408 F. Supp. 162 (D. Colo. 1975)

Facts and Issues. The plaintiffs in this case argued that the linguistic differences of Latino students in Mesa Valley School District, Number 51, were the sole cause of Latino students' poor academic performance. This obstacle thus denied them equal educational opportunity and promoted discrimination against the students.

The plaintiffs acknowledged that only a few students were affected by this problem, yet they asserted that the district violated the students' rights, which were guaranteed by the Constitution and several federal statutes. The plaintiffs requested injunctive relief against the school district's current practices and a modification of the curriculum to include a bilingual-bicultural program acceptable to the organizations representing the Latino children of Mesa Valley.

Holding. The court denied any relief for the plaintiffs and ruled in favor of the Mesa Valley School District.

Reasoning. Basing its decision on the *Keyes* (1975) decision, the court ruled that there is no constitutional right to a bilingual-bicultural education program and reaffirmed the appellate court's decision that the judiciary cannot impose such a program on a school district, even in a desegregation case. Additionally, the court declared its belief that the school district was indeed trying to overcome the language deficiencies of its language-minority students, contrary to the claims of the plaintiffs.

Finally, the court invoked what has been called the *Lau-Serna* doctrine, a guideline established by Supreme Court Justice Blackmun in the *Lau* case and supported by Judge Hill in *Serna*. The doctrine essentially rules out a Title VI violation unless a significant number exists against whom an entity has discriminated. In this case, the court said that there existed only a few language-minority children who were being denied an equal opportunity for education, and the district was taking affirmative steps to remedy that situation. Therefore, no relief was needed.

Significance of Ruling. The court clearly stated that there was no right to a bilingual-bicultural education. In addition, the court, in a caustic assault against the plaintiff, completely supported the presumption that local control is the best answer for addressing the needs of language-minority students, a policy adopted from the decision in the *Keyes* case. The court's attitude toward granting equal protection through a bilingual-bicultural education was explicit:

> If there were an Equal Protection right to bilingual/bicultural education, the needs of a single student would

give rise to that right, and our nation's schools would bankrupt themselves in meeting Equal Protection claims to bilingual educations [sic] in every conceivable language and dialect. (p. 169)

This viewpoint encountered considerable opposition through various later court decisions that determined what constitutes an equal opportunity education. Notably, these later court cases specified the distinct right to remedial language instruction for even one student who is disadvantaged because of a language barrier.

Aspira v. *New York,* 423 F. Supp. 647 (S.D. N.Y. 1976)

Facts and Issues. Under the rules of a consent decree that emerged from the decision in *Lau* and 42 U.S.C. §2000(d), New York City public school students of Hispanic origin, along with their parents and guardians, were entitled to a program of bilingual-bicultural education (*Aspira* v. *New York*, 1975). Dissatisfied with the progress of the bilingual education program, Aspira, a Puerto Rican political organization, filed suit to find the New York Board of Education in contempt of its obligations.

The decree provided for a broad bilingual program: methods of identifying those to receive bilingual instruction, specific forms of instruction in Spanish and English, the formulation of pertinent education standards, the preparation and distribution of instructional materials, the recruitment and training of staff, the procurement of suitable funding, continued consultation with plaintiffs, and periodic progress reports.

Holding. The court blamed the school district for the inadequacy of the bilingual education program and found it in contempt. It further ordered a more effective bilingual-bicultural program to be put in place.

Reasoning. The court's finding of contempt is based on the defendants' violation of their obligations under the consent decree. Specifically, the court noted the district's initial unwillingness to accept students' rights to bilingual instruction. The school district was shown to have misused its leadership and authority to ensure the program's effectiveness, thus manifesting a bad-faith effort and reflecting its lack of will to achieve substantial compliance:

> Briefly stated, the court's ultimate findings of contempt are determinations that defendants violated their obligations under the decree by failures of diligence, effective control, and steadfast purpose to effectuate the prescribed goals. The fact that goals were not achieved, or achieved only partially and tardily, is not in itself grounds for either criticizing the defendants or holding their conduct contumacious. The court is not empowered to command, any more than it can pretend for itself to achieve, performance approximating perfection. The court is obliged, however, to require substantial performance and due diligence. It is in these vital respects that today's decision must go against the defendants. As will appear, they failed steadily and repeatedly to exercise their power and authority so that those they controlled would proceed promptly and in good faith to accomplish the tasks commanded by the consent decree. This failure reflected their own lack of concentrated will to achieve substantial compliance. (p. 651)

Significance of Ruling. This decision affirmed the right of Spanish-speaking and other foreign students to have bilingual-bicultural education until they reach a level of proficiency in the English language that would facilitate equal access to education. This right was based on the *Lau* decision and §601 of the Civil Rights Act (42 U.S.C. §2000(d)). The court also found that the responsibility for ensuring effective programs of bilingual instruction fell squarely on the shoulders of the district.

Alvarado v. El Paso Independent School District, 426 F. Supp. 575 (W.D. Tex. 1976)

Facts and Issues. The impetus for this case was the concern of various groups representing Mexican-American students and parents that El Paso Independent School District had perpetuated a systematic design of race discrimination and segregation. Specifically, the plaintiffs accused the El Paso schools of failing to allow bilingual communications in parent-teacher conferences, thus denying equal educational opportunity, a guaranteed protection under the Fourteenth Amendment, to Mexican-American students.

Holding. The court dismissed the aspect of the case that specifically related to the issue of bilingual communication with the parents of Mexican-American children in the El Paso ISD.

Reasoning. The court noted that the issue of bilingual communication was moot because any discriminatory effects of past practices were eased through current school policy. El Paso ISD policy was, at the time of the case, to distribute report cards for elementary school children in both English and Spanish. Also, the court noted the district's implementation of various other, unnamed, practices promoting bilingual communication with parents.

Significance of Ruling. This case is helpful in understanding the basic philosophy of the district court system as it relates to bilingual issues. It seems that the court wholeheartedly supported the use of bilingual communications with parents. It is further evident that the court's refusal to modify the district's practice indicates its unwillingness to meddle in district policy without significant cause. This promotes the idea other courts have advanced that the individual school district and its community are better policy makers than the judicial system.

Armstrong v. *O'Connell,* 74 F.R.D. 429 (E.D. Wis. 1977)

Facts and Issues. This case centered on the request of the City-Wide Bilingual Bicultural Parent Advisory Committee and various Latino students to intervene in a desegregation case as representatives of a plaintiff class comprised of Latino students enrolled in bilingual programs in the Milwaukee public school system. This request was a result of the desegregation lawsuit *Amos* v. *Board of*

City of Milwaukee (1976). In 1976 the court determined that the Milwaukee School District had intentionally maintained a segregated school system and thus was ordered to formulate remediation plans. The court certified two plaintiff classes, one consisting of all black students and the other consisting of all non-black students. The Hispanic pupils were classified as members of the non-black class.

During the remaining two years of the desegregation order, the district advised the court of its adoption of a statement titled, "Major Issues, Assurances, and Legal Principles Affecting the Hispanic Pupil During Desegregation Efforts," and the plaintiffs sought to intervene in the case.

Holding. The court ruled against the plaintiffs and denied their motion to intervene in the remediation of the desegregation plan as outlined in the *Amos* case.

Reasoning. The court ruled that the defendant school district had not demonstrated any impairment of the interests of the parent advisory committee with respect to the bilingual-bicultural program. The motion to intervene to protect the bilingual-bicultural program was considered premature because the school district had not manifested any signs of denying an equal educational opportunity to language-minority students. It was found that quite the opposite was the reality.

The court cited the Fifth Circuit opinion that "no remedy for the dual system can be acceptable if it operates to deprive members of a third ethnic group of the benefits of equal educational opportunity" (*United States* v. *Texas Education Agency*, 1972). Within that context, the court indicated that the final remedial order of the *Amos* decision did not prevent the defendants from giving Hispanic students priority over other non-black students in assignment to schools with bilingual-bicultural programs. Quite the opposite was the case. In the court's final remedial order, paragraph 3(j) states:

> Nothing in this order is intended to prevent defendants from designating Hispanic students, native Americans, and

other minority students as separate minority populations and according them priority over other non-black students in assignment to schools with programs designed to meet their special needs. (p. 432)

Moreover, the guidelines described in the order were explicitly liberal in order to give the school district enough flexibility to handle various concerns, such as bilingual-bicultural programs. The court also pointed out that the defendant school district seemed to have recognized the legality of bilingual-bicultural programs and to have expressed a commitment to continue such programs.

Significance of Ruling. The court decided that an intervention by a third ethnic class, such as the Hispanic plaintiffs in this case, was in some instances appropriate, as exemplified through the Texas decision from 1972. However, when district policy clearly favors the language-minority population, the court must refuse any request for intervention in a desegregation case.

Notably, within the context of this case, the school board asserted its commitment to serving the needs of language-minority students through a document titled, "Major Issues, Assurances, and Legal Principles Affecting the Hispanic Pupil During Desegregation Efforts." Through this document, the district promoted the idea that bilingual-bicultural programs are not only required by federal law and Wisconsin state law, but also are required by educational and social necessity:

> Bilingual-bicultural education and integration are compatible and feasible. Both efforts are attempts at providing equality of education opportunity for pupils. Bilingual-bicultural education programs are to enhance integration efforts as opposed to having a segregative effect. Social and cultural interaction are [sic] further assets to language and cultural maintenance. (p. 432)

Cintron v. *Brentwood,* 455 F. Supp. 57 (E.D. N.Y. 1978)

Facts and Issues. Plaintiffs alleged that the Brentwood School District was in violation of Title VI of the Civil Rights Act and the Equal Educational Opportunity Act of 1974 by restructuring its transitional bilingual education program, known as Project Avelino, to what the district called Plan V. Project Avelino, which at the time of this case had 460 children, was a transitional bilingual education program designed to increase the use of English while gradually decreasing the use of Spanish until the sixth grade, when all courses would be taught in English. Bilingual teachers and their aides taught the bilingual classes, which included some coursework in Latin American culture and history. Since the inception of Project Avelino to the time of litigation, no students had transferred from the bilingual program to the full English program. Furthermore, students in Project Avelino were segregated, staying in the same classroom except for physical education and lunch.

The program known as Plan V would have functioned in seven elementary schools in the district, offering an English-as-a-second-language and Latin American cultural program run in much the same manner as Project Avelino. One addition of note would have been a Spanish basic skills room for remediation. Students would have attended monolingual English classes, and bilingual teachers there would offer remedial help by explaining in Spanish the subject matter covered.

Under both plans, the method for identifying language-minority students was initiated in kindergarten through registration by a Spanish-speaking social worker or psychologist. Once identified, the child's parents had the option of choosing a class taught in English, an English for speakers of other languages (ESOL) program, or a bilingual program. Significantly, there did not exist a reliable method for identifying language-minority students in the upper grades.

Holding. Basing its decision on violations of the Bilingual Education Act (20 U.S.C. 880(b)), the Lau Remedies, the Equal Educational Opportunity Act (20 U.S.C. §1703(f)), and §601 of the Civil Rights Act (42 U.S.C. §2000(d)), the court held that both Project Avelino and Plan V were deficient in meeting the needs of the district's language-minority students. The court ordered the district to revise its bilingual education plan to parallel the requirements set forth in the Lau Guidelines and the EEOA.

Reasoning. Project Avelino was found to violate the Equal Educational Opportunity Act through the Lau Guidelines. School officials conceded that in Project Avelino, Spanish-speaking students were kept separate and apart from English-speaking students in music and art. Project Avelino also was conducted as a maintenance program, and school officials discouraged students from transferring out of the program. There was no procedure for removing students who reached the level of proficiency in the English language that would enable them to understand regular English instruction.

Plan V was deficient in that the plan did not clearly indicate the manner of identifying students who are deficient in the English language. Thus it violated provisions in the Bilingual Education Act (20 U.S.C. §880(b)), the Equal Educational Opportunity Act (20 U.S.C. §1703(f)), and §601 of the Civil Rights Act (42 U.S.C. §2000(d)). The court elaborated its point with the following opinion:

> While integration is encouraged, there is no assurance that language deficient children in the upper grades will be identified. If they are, there is the continued threat of insufficient remedial assistance. For if a child cannot comprehend principles of math or science taught in the English homeroom, he will not be able to explain his or her problem to the bilingual teacher in the Spanish basic skills room who is expected to provide remedial help. Moreover, children continually in need of remedial assistance, who might spend more time in the basic skills room than they are scheduled for, run the risk of missing planned instruction, thus further retarding their educational progress. (p. 63)

Significance of Ruling. This case presented the district court's plan for effectively meeting the requirements of the EEOA through the Lau Guidelines. The plan to replace Project Avelino, which appeared to be the court's dream remedy for such language policy cases, was ordered to contain specific methods for identifying language-minority children and for monitoring the progress of such children to ascertain achievement levels and proficiency in the English language. Furthermore, the plan, which would be bilingual-bicultural, also was mandated to have a training component for bilingual teachers and bilingual aides and a method for transferring students out of the program when the necessary level of English proficiency was reached. The court ordered that the plan should not isolate children into racially or ethnically identifiable classes, but should encourage contact between non-English- and English-speaking children in all but subject matter instruction.

Rios v. *Read,* 480 F. Supp. 14 (E.D. N.Y. 1978)

Facts and Issues. Several Puerto Rican parents in the Patchogue-Medford School District brought action against the district on behalf of their children. The parents claimed that their children's language deficiencies hindered their education, thus denying them equal educational opportunity guaranteed by §601 of the Civil Rights Act (42 U.S.C. §2000(d)) and the Equal Protection Clause of the Fourteenth Amendment. Only 186 of the approximately 800 Latino students participated in the bilingual education program, whose nature was transitional. The district asserted that the program was primarily an ESL program with bilingual and bicultural elements that would enhance the achievement level of language-minority students. Plaintiffs complained that this transitional bilingual education program was actually counterproductive and harmful to the students.

Holding. The court ruled that the district's transitional bilingual education program did not go far enough to remedy the language barrier faced by the language-minority students.

Reasoning. Mentioning the mandate in 20 U.S.C. §1703(f), the court ruled that the district's bilingual education program did not go far enough to remedy the education problems faced by language-minority students. The court stated:

> A denial of educational opportunities to a child in the first years of schooling is not justified by demonstrating that the educational program employed will teach the child English sooner than programs comprised of more extensive Spanish instruction. While the District's goal of teaching Hispanic children the English language is certainly proper, it cannot be allowed to compromise a student's right to meaningful education before proficiency in English is obtained. (p. 23)

Declaring that the district's bilingual education policy violated the students' rights of equal educational opportunity, the court ruled that the district was to take a proactive move toward providing the students with an effective ESL and bilingual program. The district also was to ensure not only that all language-minority students be identified and placed in the program, but also that all such students should remain in the program until English-language proficiency was met to the level at which students could be instructed with English-speaking students of the same intelligence.

Significance of Ruling. The court took a bold position in this case by actually mandating a bilingual education program, something other courts have ruled is not necessary to remedy discrimination practices against language-minority students.

The court indicated that it had the inherent power to order relief and thus implemented what it called "equitable power" to ensure language-minority children a meaningful education. The court also required that a limited bicultural program be put in place so as to enhance the children's learning ability. However, the court warned that this program was not to be carried out indefinitely. The court asserted that the goal was to ensure equal educational opportunity, not to establish a bilingual society.

Guadalupe Org. Inc. v. *Tempe Elem. Sch. Dist.,* 587 F.2d 1022 (9th Cir. 1978)

Facts and Issues. Appellants were Mexican-American and Yaqui Indian elementary school children living in the community of Guadalupe, Arizona, a semirural community of approximately 5,000 people, most of whom were Mexican American or Yaqui. The children and their representatives alleged that the school district failed to provide bilingual instruction that took into account the special education needs of Mexican-American and Yaqui students, failed to hire enough teachers of Mexican-American or Yaqui descent who could adequately teach bilingual courses and effectively relate to the cultural needs of the students, failed to structure a curriculum that took into account the children's particular needs, and failed to structure a curriculum that reflected the historical contributions of the children's ancestors to Arizona and the United States. The plaintiffs claimed that a resolution to these complaints were justified by the Fourteenth Amendment's Equal Protection Clause, §601 of the Civil Rights Act of 1964 (42 U.S.C. §2000(d)), and §1703(f), the equal educational opportunity clause.

Holding. The court denied the plaintiffs' appeal in favor of the Tempe School District.

Reasoning. The court reasoned that since the appellants alleged no intentional discrimination and readily acknowledged that the remedial instruction in English was sufficient to allow Mexican-American and Yaqui students to participate effectively in the education program, then no violation of the Equal Educational Opportunity Act existed.

Furthermore, the court said that failure to do more than what is minimally required does not qualify as a discriminatory course of conduct condemned by the Equal Protection clause. The decision in *San Antonio* v. *Rodriguez* (1973) addressed the nature of what constitutes an appropriate education: one that is minimally effective to enable participation in the American political process. Assuming adequate remedial instruction, education in English reflecting only American culture and values is not a discriminatory course of conduct.

This court rejected claims filed under § 601 of the Civil Rights Act because it found no discrimination. It based this finding on the plaintiffs' admission that the district complied with guidelines set forth by *Lau*.

Significance of Ruling. This case is a key ruling in which this federal court overturned the mandate in *Serna*, which ordered districts to have a bilingual-bicultural program to achieve equal educational opportunity. Specifically, this court ruled that there does not exist a constitutional right to a bilingual-bicultural program in the public schools. It also rejected the idea that a bilingual-bicultural education program was mandated by §1703(f) of the Equal Educational Opportunity Act, which simply requires districts to "take appropriate action to overcome language barriers that impede equal participation by its students in its instructional programs." The court pointed out that there is no prohibition against a bilingual-bicultural program either, for it is up to the people of the community to decide such matters.

Deerfield v. *Ipswich Board of Education*, 468 F. Supp. 1219 (N.D. S.D. 1979)

Facts and Issues. Based on a charge of religious discrimination by the Ipswich School District and the charge that the district violated the Equal Educational Opportunity Act and §601 of the Civil Rights Act, the plaintiffs requested that the court order the Ipswich Board of Education to establish and organize a school at or near the Deerfield Hutterite Colony, an Anabaptist-based religious community that speaks Tyrolean German.

Tyrolean German is an oral language that does not exist in a written form. Not only are the Hutterites the only group to speak Tyrolean German, they are unable to write in their native and dominant language because a written form of the language is nonexistent. The Hutterites preserve their history and sermons in High German and conduct their religious services in that language. The Hutterites do not use High German on a regular basis other than in their religious services. They do not use it as a means of written communication. According to the findings of the court, the Hutterites can read and understand the familiar passages of sermons written in High German but, other than their preachers, few, if any, have the ability to use it for everyday purposes.

The Hutterite community discourages the use of English. It is not until the first grade that Hutterite children are exposed to the English language. Furthermore, because of their religion, the Hutterites have objected to education beyond the eighth grade. One exception is a certain Levi Tschetter Sr., who at the time of this case was the only Hutterite in the United States who was a qualified school teacher. Mr. Tschetter was one of only a few Hutterites who had graduated from college. Teachers and older Hutterite children, who served as interpreters, taught students in Hutterite schools. These interpreters were students in the seventh or eighth grades who were proficient in English.

Because of widespread consolidation efforts, Deerfield children of the Hutterite community had been students of various South Dakota school districts. The Hutterites opposed any effort to have their children bused to Ipswich, regardless of the type of bilingual-bicultural program that the school board would have implemented. Their fear was not only that the children would be exposed to "worldly goods and ideas in Ipswich," but also that "their religious beliefs would be subjected to public question and criticism" (p. 1225). The issue of this case is whether the Deerfield plaintiffs had the right to a bilingual program established in their colony.

Holding. The court rejected all of the claims held by the plaintiffs and denied the request by the plaintiffs to have the Ipswich School District organize a school at the Deerfield Colony.

Reasoning. The court stated that since there is no constitutional duty imposed by the Equal Protection Clause to provide bilingual-bicultural education within the Hutterite colony, the community must accept the wishes of the Ipswich School District.

According to the court, the evidence showed that a successful bilingual-bicultural program could be established in Ipswich, which would be to the benefit of the Hutterite children, who could be bused into town. The court stated that the education of the children at the Hutterite colony was not in the children's best interest; education at a school located in town, where adequate facilities and teaching personnel were centrally located, would be better. The court also rejected the Hutterite supposition that their religious freedom would be impinged if they were not provided with a segregated religious community school.

> What the Hutterites are seeking is a segregated or a separate school because of what are primarily religious and cultural reasons. The reasons being, of course, the desire to keep the Colony children separated from the world. The Hutterites' beliefs are such that they feel contact with worldly goods and ideas will keep them from eternal salvation. The Board has no right to prevent the Hutterites from practicing their firmly held religious beliefs. This Court strongly disagrees with the plaintiffs' contention that *Yoder* supports their case. The *Yoder* case does not stand for the proposition that if a religious group feels strongly about its religious tenets and wishes its children segregated from the world, it can force the state to set up and pay for a separate school for the children. (p. 1228)

Significance of Ruling. This case established that a school district is not required by the Fourteenth Amendment, 20 U.S.C. §1703(f) (EEOA), or 42 U.S.C. §2000(d) to establish a bilingual-bicultural program or even a school for students for a religious community when adequate programs and facilities already exist within the district. It also reaffirmed the *San Antonio* v. *Rodriguez* (1973) decision, in which the Supreme Court ruled that there is no fundamental right to an education.

Martin Luther King Jr. Elementary School Children et al. v. Ann Arbor School District, 473 F. Supp. 1371 (E.D. Mich. 1979)

Facts and Issues. Eleven black children brought suit against the school board, asserting discrimination based on equal protection guaranteed by 20 U.S.C. §1703(f) (EEOA). The children charged that they spoke a version of so-called black English, otherwise known as Ebonics, as their community and home language, which impeded their equal participation in the education process and that the school had not taken appropriate action to overcome the barrier. The inaction of the district was alleged to be the district's failure to educate the black children in standard English.

The district court indicated that this case was an effort to require the school district to take appropriate action to teach the black children to read in standard English. Witnesses before the court testified that Ebonics is a language system that differs significantly from standard English and had been used at some time by 80% of the black people of this country. This dialect is especially prevalent in areas where there are concentrations of black people, and it contains aspects of Southern dialect that are used largely by black people in their casual conversation and informal talk. In particular, the plaintiff children not only used this so-called black English in their informal conversations at home, but also at school.

Although the children in this case did at times speak Ebonics at home, they also understood standard English in the school and at home. The teachers in the school had no difficulty in understanding the students or their parents in the school setting, and the children could understand the teachers and other children in that setting. In other words, there was no barrier to understanding caused by the language. The language barrier was caused by the failure to take into account the home language of the children during instruction of standard English.

Holding. The court ruled in favor of the children and mandated affirmative steps to be taken by the school district to identify children speaking black English and to use that knowledge in teaching students how to read standard English.

Reasoning. The facts in this case indicated that these children had not developed reading skills, and the failure to develop these skills impeded equal participation in the instructional program. In addition, the court indicated that the school board had not taken steps to help the teachers understand the problem, to provide them with knowledge about the children's use of Ebonics, and to suggest ways and means of using that knowledge to more effectively teach the students to read. Because of the failure of the school board to help its teachers learn about the existence of the black English dialect as a home and community language of many black students and to suggest to those same teachers ways and means of using that knowledge in teaching the black children certain literacy skills in connection with reading standard English, the court ruled in favor of the plaintiffs. Specifically, the court ordered the school board to take steps to help its teachers recognize the home language of the students and to use that knowledge in their attempts to teach reading skills in standard English.

Significance of Ruling. Although the court ruled in favor of the children, it pointed out that it would not be appropriate to classify the difference between black and standard English as a language barrier. Instead, it classified the differences as a cultural, economic, and social problem.

A notable discussion in this case concerned the applicability of the EEOA and included comments by President Nixon urging enactment of the law. The President had stated that this law would provide "a broader base on which to decide future cases" and "standards for all school districts throughout the Nation, as the basic requirements for carrying out, in the field of public education, the Constitutional guarantee that each person shall have equal protection of the laws" (118 Cong. Rec. 8931, 1972).

In re Alien Children Education Litigation, 501 F. Supp. 544 (S.D. Tex. 1980)

Facts and Issues. The issue in this court was a Texas law that prohibited the use of state funds to educate "persons who are not citizens of the United States or 'legally admitted aliens'" (Tex. Educ. Code Ann. 2 §21.031). The law permitted local school districts to exclude undocumented children from the public schools.

A Compendium of Court Decisions

Plaintiffs asserted that the statute denied them equal protection guaranteed by the Fourteenth Amendment.

Holding. The court ruled in favor of the alien children's petition and submitted an order to enjoin the Texas law. With respect to the issue, the court offered an implicit opinion that Texas school districts have a hollow complaint on their burden of providing education, particularly bilingual education, to undocumented alien children.

Reasoning. Citing constitutional precedent, the court ruled that because the Texas government took it upon itself to provide education services in its state, it could not deny that education to a discrete group of children absent sufficient justification. It further offered what it called "practical concerns":

> Another aspect of this public question bears emphasis. As residents of a country which is reexamining its history and future as a home for persons of all nationalities and cultures, we cannot forget the role that the public schools have played providing unity to our community of immigrants. To insure that we do not fractionalize into a country of ethnic groups without shared goals and ideals, all of our social and public institutions must work to profit from our cultural diversity while working toward common interests. The institution which must continue to assume the greatest responsibility is the public school. We must remember that we strive to form a more perfect union and that the union comprises individuals. Our endeavor to create such a society will be frustrated if we deny a discrete group of children the chance to develop their individuality. The public schools are the essential element in that development. (p. 596)

The court rejected the idea that educating undocumented alien children would place an insurmountable burden on Texas school districts. Although the state presented evidence that there was a shortage of qualified bilingual teachers in some school districts, which would strain each of those district's resources, the court also heard expert testimony describing methods and techniques available to offset the shortage of bilingual teachers. The court did not deny that many Texas school districts would encounter difficulty providing equal educational opportunity to all children, even alien, language-minority children. However, the court found no need to exclude these children in order to protect other children in the state.

The court further indicated that various sources of funds were available to help states meet the bilingual education needs of all students. Some of those sources included state funds for bilingual education and federal funds authorized by the Bilingual Education Act, Title I of the Elementary and Secondary Education Act, and the Emergency School Aid Act bilingual grants, not to mention Title I Migrant Education funds. The court pointed out that there had been no restrictions on using these funds to educate alien children. Therefore, the state had significant resources on which to draw for help in addressing its burden of providing the alien children with an equal educational opportunity.

Significance of Ruling. In a precursor to the later Supreme Court case, *Plyler* v. *Doe* (1982), this court offered a salient opinion regarding the education of alien children. It stressed that many resources have been available, both through the state and federal governments, to provide an equal educational opportunity, especially with regard to language remediation services, to all children, regardless of their condition or citizenship status. The court's empathy with the situation of the undocumented children was affirmed in the conclusion from a quote by Bishop John Edward McCarthy:

> We are keeping certain people poor, and what we are manufacturing now is a monumental social cost to our society ten and fifteen and twenty years from now. . . . We are manufacturing ignorance; to be ignorant in society is to be nonproductive; to be nonproductive means for many instances to be forced into a state of crime. . . . Whether it be right now in the form of modest increases in tuition, in public school operating cost, or . . . in terms of social cost . . . fifteen years from now, we will pay this bill. (Cong. Rec. Vol. VII, 124-25)

U.S. v. *Texas*, 506 F. Supp. 405 (E.D. Tex. 1981), rev'd, 680 F.2d 356 (1982)

Facts and Issues. This case was originally a desegregation case brought against the Texas Education Agency (TEA) in 1970. The U.S. Department of Justice claimed that the TEA failed to properly oversee local school district efforts to desegregate their schools. In 1971 a federal court ordered the agency to develop and implement a plan for ensuring the success of desegregation efforts statewide. Although the TEA, under the authority of a component of that court order known as Section G, prepared an 86-page report with a 17-page section on "Alternative Programs to Improve Curriculum for Minority Students," there were claims that the agency was not actually doing anything to remedy the plight of its language-minority students. However, according to the court order, submitting these reports was the only thing the agency had been required to do. No other specific actions were mandated by the order, such as directing TEA to address the learning problems of language-minority students.

In 1972 several action groups, including the GI Forum and the League of Latin American Citizens, moved to intervene in the Texas matter. The motion specifically sought to require the enforcement of Section G of the 1971 order and requested supplemental relief by the TEA for Mexican-American students in Texas who were classified as language minorities. The specific relief, with the purpose of ensuring equal educational opportunity for these students, was the requirement of bilingual instruction and compensatory programs. The subsequent challenge to the TEA's efforts claimed violations under Title VI of the Civil Rights Act, the Equal Protection Clause of the Fourteenth Amendment, and §1703 of the Equal Educational Opportunity Act of 1974. Although significant findings were made in this case, a 1982 appeal claimed that the court's order was rendered moot by the passage of a bilingual education statute by the Texas legislature (Bilingual and Special Language Programs Act of Texas, 1981).

Holding. The 1981 court denied the plaintiffs' claim for relief as a means of enforcing Section G of the 1971 court order. The court denied relief for the Mexican-American children's claims of discrimination under Title VI of the Civil Rights Act and the Equal Protection Clause of the Fourteenth Amendment. The court granted relief for the plaintiffs under 20 U.S.C. §1703 (Equal Educational Opportunity Act of 1974).

The appeals court overturned the 1981 decision, rendering it moot.

Reasoning. Both the Supreme Court and the Fifth Court of Appeals had classified Mexican-American children as a distinct ethnic class. Moreover, discrimination against Mexican-American students in Texas had been described as acute and invidious. The segregation of Mexican Americans was a historical fact in Texas public schools, beginning in the early part of the 20th century with the establishment of so-called Mexican schools in the Rio Grande Valley. The court found that the state and local education agencies justified this practice of segregation on the basis that Mexican-American children spoke little English and often arrived late in the school year because their families engaged in migrant labor. However, as the court noted, no attempt was made to meet the special education needs of these language-minority children, for these segregated schools were shown to be inferior to schools provided for non-minority students. This intolerance also was manifested in the state's "no Spanish" policy, which punished any student who spoke any language other than English at school. This rule was strictly enforced until 1968.

The state of Texas repealed the 1918 "English only" law in 1969 and permitted bilingual education by local school districts. In 1973 the state legislature enacted the Texas Bilingual Education Act, voicing support for compensatory bilingual education programs. In 1975 the Texas legislature amended the law to limit bilingual education programs to early elementary grades. The court found that severe imperfections were present in the state's remedial plans:

> Serious flaws permeate every aspect of the state's effort. Required program content, described in detail by state law and regulation, is frequently ignored by local school districts. The scanty coverage of the state's bilingual program leaves tens of thousands of Mexican-American children without the compensatory help they require to function effectively as students. Identification of limited English proficiency students by local school districts is unreliable and unverified. Criteria for transferring students out of bilingual programs and into all-English classrooms are fixed far too low to ensure that all vestiges of discrimination have been removed before relief is cut off. Finally, the state has failed to monitor local bilingual programs in a thorough and diligent manner or to enforce applicable laws and regulations through the imposition of sanctions in appropriate circumstances. Since the defendants have not remedied these serious deficiencies, meaningful relief for the victims of unlawful discrimination must be instituted by court decree. (p. 427)

The court ruled against the Mexican-American students with respect to their claim under the Equal Protection Clause and Title VI of the Civil Rights Act.

> It is unquestionable that the defendants' refusal to provide bilingual instruction at all grade levels for all children of limited-English proficiency has effected a disproportionate impact upon the state's Mexican-American ethnic minority. But there is no evidence that the state's recent policies, isolated from the long history of purposeful discrimination, were themselves designed with the intent of perpetuating that discrimination. The state's existing program of remedial instruction for these disadvantaged children may be inadequate, but it is not, in itself, discriminatory. In the absence of purposeful discrimination, the state's failure to provide comprehensive bilingual instruction for all Mexican-American students who need it does not, apart from the past de jure discrimination suffered by that ethnic group, constitute an independent violation of the Equal Protection Clause. Since Title VI has now been deemed coextensive with the

Fourteenth Amendment, neither has there been a violation of that statute. (p. 430)

Regarding 20 U.S.C. §1703(f), commonly called the Equal Educational Opportunity Clause, the court noted that, unlike challenges based on Title VI or the Fourteenth Amendment, a finding of discriminatory intent or purpose did not have to be found. The clause simply refers to any failure by a local education agency to overcome the language barrier of any student, regardless of how the barrier originated or why the agency has neglected to take corrective measures. Because of this test, the court found that the TEA was severely lacking in its efforts to overcome the language barriers of Mexican-American students. However, as it made this claim, the court elaborated on several salient points regarding bilingual education:

> It is true that bilingual instruction per se is not required by § 1703(f) or any other provision of law. If the defendants here had implemented another type of program which effectively overcame the language barriers of Mexican-American students and enabled them to participate equally in the school curriculum, without using bilingual instruction of any kind, such a course would constitute "appropriate action" and preclude statutory relief. . . . The evidence also demonstrated that bilingual instruction is uniquely suited to meet the needs of the state's Spanish-speaking students. Therefore, the defendants will be required to take further steps, including additional bilingual instruction, if needed, to satisfy their affirmative obligation under the statute and enforce the right of these linguistically deprived children to equal educational opportunity. (p. 433)

In 1981 the district court ordered the school to provide bilingual-bicultural education for the students; but soon after, the Texas legislature passed comprehensive new legislation to address many of the issues noted by the court. The Fifth Court of Appeals reversed the district court's decision in 1982 on the basis that the 1981 Texas law, which required bilingual education in elementary school districts, rendered this earlier Texas case moot.

Significance of Ruling. Voicing strong support of 20 U.S.C. §1703(f) but not requiring bilingual education as a means to overcome language barriers was a key point of this opinion. The court's opinion stressed that bilingual education in and of itself should only be transitional in nature, to be provided only as long as needed to transition language-minority students into all-English classrooms. Furthermore, this decision affirmed the obligation to prove discriminatory intent to win a case based on 42 U.S.C. §2000(d) (Title VI of the Civil Rights Act) and the Equal Protection Clause of the Fourteenth Amendment.

Evans v. *Buchanan*, 512 F. Supp. 839 (D. Del. 1981)

Facts and Issues. This was a complex desegregation case dating back to 1976. During the case, a considerable number of Latino plaintiffs raised a claim concerning the enforceability of pupil assignment requirements mandated in earlier desegregation orders. They argued that eligible Hispanic students' access to a bilingual education would be jeopardized by a conflict between the desegregation regulations and a state statute.

The regulation in question required what was called District 2 to house and administer the bilingual program originally established in the 1978 decree. To permit enrollment of eligible pupils not resident in District 2, the regulations bound the affected districts to exercise their statutory powers to provide for student transfers and to raise the necessary tuition payments. The question that had arisen was whether the regulation's direct mandate to approve bilingual students' transfers was a proper exercise of the state board's regulatory power or an unenforceable violation of the local districts' statutory prerogative.

Holding. The court refused to resolve the matter.

Reasoning. The court based its decision on the ambiguity of the state law, which was deemed to be unclear in this matter. The court ruled that the state should be the entity making such a decision.

Significance of Ruling. This case exemplifies the unwillingness of the court to interpose itself into the internal affairs of the state.

In the concluding part of the brief, the court applauded the state for setting forth its own plan for desegregation and emphasized the need for states to arrive at their own solutions without having to be ordered to do so by judicial decree.

Idaho Migrant Council v. *Board of Education,* 647 F.2d 69 (9th Cir. 1981)

Facts and Issues. The Idaho Migrant Council, a nonprofit corporation representing Idaho public school students with limited-English language proficiency, filed suit against the Idaho State Department and Board of Education, charging that the agencies violated federal law because they failed to ensure that local school districts were providing language-minority students in Idaho equal educational opportunity. A district court had granted summary judgment for the department and board of education on the basis that, under Idaho state law, the agencies were not empowered to supervise compliance with federal law by the local school districts.

Holding. The court reversed the earlier district court decision and found that the defendant agencies were indeed responsible for ensuring that school districts were in compliance of the Equal Educational Opportunity Act and the Civil Rights Act of 1964.

Reasoning. The court concluded that both Idaho state law and federal law required the state education agencies to supervise local districts. Specifically, the language of 20 U.S.C. §1703 et seq. explicitly states that the state cannot deny equal educational opportunity "by the failure of an *educational agency* [italics added] to take appropriate action to overcome language barriers that impede equal participation by its students in its instructional programs." Furthermore, the obligation is contractual under 42 U.S.C. §2000(d) (Title VI of the Civil Rights Act of 1964) by virtue of the state's acceptance of federal funds. The relevant statute clearly states, "[n]o person in the United States shall, on the ground of race, color, or national origin, be excluded from participation in, be denied the benefits of, or be subjected to discrimination under any program or activity *receiving Federal financial assistance* [italics added]."

Significance of Ruling. Under the authority of federal statutory law, this case asserted the obligation of the state and its underlying education agencies for ensuring that local districts provide equal opportunities for education and freedom from discrimination.

Castañeda v. *Pickard,* 648 F.2d 989 (5th Cir. 1981)

Facts and Issues. Mexican-American children and their parents appealed a lower court decision concerning their lawsuit against the Raymondville, Texas, Independent School District (RISD) for engaging in policies of racial discrimination, which deprived the plaintiffs of certain constitutional rights related to the Fourteenth Amendment, Equal Educational Opportunity Act of 1974, and Title VI of the Civil Rights Act of 1964. Specifically, the students alleged the school district illegally discriminated against them by using an ability grouping system for classroom assignments, which was based on classroom segregation; by discriminating against Mexican Americans in the hiring of staff and faculty; and by failing to implement adequate bilingual education to overcome the language barriers that hamper the students' equal participation in the education program of the district.

Holding. The court ruled against the Castañeda party, concluding that the RISD had not violated Title VI of the Civil Rights Act. The issue of the district's violating the Equal Protection Clause of the Fourteenth Amendment and the EEOA were remanded and later heard again by this same court in *Castañeda II* (*Castañeda* v. *Pickard*, 1986), which ruled that there existed no violations of either the EEOA or the Equal Protection Clause.

Reasoning. Within the frame of *Castañeda*, the court pointed out that Congress amended the Elementary and Secondary Education Act in 1974, enacting both the Equal Educational Opportunity Act of 1974 (EEOA) and the Bilingual Education Act

(BEA) and specifying that states must take appropriate action to remediate limited-English proficient (LEP) students (20 U.S.C. §1703(f)). According to the court, the use of the term "appropriate action," rather than "bilingual education," indicated that Congress "intended to leave state and local educational authorities a substantial amount of latitude in choosing the programs and techniques they would use to meet their obligations under the EEOA," while at the same time ensuring that "schools made a genuine and good faith effort, consistent with local circumstances and resources, to remedy the language deficiencies of their students" (p. 1009). Under §1703 et. seq. of the EEOA, education agencies not only have an obligation to overcome the direct obstacle to learning that the language barrier itself poses, but also have a duty to provide limited-English-speaking students with assistance in other areas of the curriculum where their equal participation may be impaired because of the language remediation program. Also, §1703 et. seq. allows schools to determine the sequence and manner in which limited-English-proficient students handle the challenge of undergoing English instruction, as well as maintaining instruction in other curricular activities. The court further pointed out that Congress had provided the judicial branch with almost no guidance in determining if a school district's language remediation efforts were appropriate. The Fifth Circuit judges complained that the courts are:

> confronted with a type of task which federal courts are ill equipped to perform and which we are often criticized for undertaking prescribing substantive standards and policies for institutions whose governance is properly reserved to other levels and branches of our government, which are better able to assimilate and access the knowledge of professionals in the field. (p. 1009)

Furthermore, the appeals court explained that, while §1703 et. seq. requires school districts to take appropriate action, it does not require a program of bilingual education.

> We do not believe that Congress, at the time it adopted the EEOA, intended to require local educational authorities to

adopt any particular type of language remediation program. At the same time Congress enacted the EEOA, it passed the Bilingual Education Act of 1974. . . . We note that although Congress enacted both the Bilingual Education Act and the EEOA as part of the 1974 amendments to the Elementary and Secondary Education Act, Congress, in describing the remedial obligation it sought to impose on the states in the EEOA, did not specify that a state must provide a program of "bilingual education" to all limited-English speaking students. (p. 1008-09)

However, this explanation did not absolve school districts of any responsibility from attempting to address the problem of language barriers. The court indicated that although language-minority students may have to be segregated for a time because of a language remediation program, the ultimate goal of such a program would be to integrate the child into the English-language program as soon as possible. According to the court, it was clear that Congress intended for schools to make genuine, good faith efforts to remedy language deficiencies.

The *Castañeda* court devised a three-part test designed "to fulfill the responsibility Congress has assigned to us without unduly substituting our educational values and theories for the educational and political decisions reserved to state or local school authorities or the expert knowledge of educators" (p. 1009). According to the court, for a bilingual education program to be considered an appropriate action under §1703 et. seq., a school must show that: 1) it "is pursuing a program informed by educational theory recognized as sound by some experts in the field or, at least, deemed a legitimate experimental strategy"; 2) the programs and practices actually used by a school are "reasonably calculated to implement effectively the educational theory adopted by the school"; and 3) the program "produce[s] results indicating that the language barriers confronting students are actually being overcome" (pp. 1009-10).

The *Castañeda* plaintiffs went to trial again on remand, the case being known later as *Castañeda II*, amending their complaint to name the Texas Education Agency (TEA) as a defendant. The plaintiffs alleged the TEA had failed to fulfill its duty to ensure that plaintiffs were not subjected to discriminatory practices through the use of state or federal funds and that an adequate bilingual program was implemented by RISD. The district and appeals court again ruled in favor of the RISD, noting that no violations of the Equal Protection Clause or the EEOA were evident (*Castañeda* v. *Pickard*, 1986).

Significance of Ruling. The court rejected the plaintiff's application of the Lau Guidelines and subsequently questioned the continuing relevance of *Lau* itself to the area of bilingual education. It cited *Washington* v. *Davis* (1976), an employment discrimination case, which held that an official act that has a racially disproportionate effect is not unconstitutional unless it reflects a discriminatory purpose, rather than simply a disparate impact. Furthermore, concerning the case *University of California Regents* v. *Bakke* (1978), the Supreme Court interpreted Title VI of the Civil Rights Act to be coextensive with the Equal Protection Clause. Although the Supreme Court did not overrule *Lau* in *Bakke*, it did explicitly assert that Title VI, like the Equal Protection Clause, is violated only by conduct intended to discriminate and not by conduct that has a differential effect on persons of different races.

Probably the most significant aspect of this case was the introduction of the three-prong *Castañeda* test, which has been used in many other language education policy cases. A complete description of the test follows:

> In a case such as this one in which the appropriateness of a particular school system's language remediation program is challenged under § 1703(f), we believe that the responsibility of the federal court is threefold.
>
> First, the court must examine carefully the evidence the record contains concerning the soundness of the educational theory or principles upon which the challenged program is based.
>
> This, of course, is not to be done with any eye toward discerning the relative merits of sound but competing bodies of

expert educational opinion, for choosing between sound but competing theories is properly left to the educators and public officials charged with responsibility for directing the educational policy of a school system. The state of the art in the area of language remediation may well be such that respected authorities legitimately differ as to the best type of educational program for limited-English speaking students and we do not believe that Congress in enacting § 1703(f) intended to make the resolution of these differences the province of federal courts. The court's responsibility, insofar as educational theory is concerned, is only to ascertain that a school system is pursuing a program informed by an educational theory recognized as sound by some experts in the field or, at least, deemed a legitimate experimental strategy.

The court's second inquiry would be whether the programs and practices actually used by a school system are reasonably calculated to implement effectively the educational theory adopted by the school. We do not believe that it may fairly be said that a school system is taking appropriate action to remedy language barriers if, despite the adoption of a promising theory, the system fails to follow through with practices, resources and personnel necessary to transform the theory into reality.

Finally, a determination that a school system has adopted a sound program for alleviating the language barriers impeding the educational progress of some of its students and made bona fide efforts to make the program work does not necessarily end the court's inquiry into the appropriateness of the system's actions. If a school's program, although premised on a legitimate educational theory and implemented through the use of adequate techniques, fails, after being employed for a period of time sufficient to give the plan a legitimate trial, to produce results indicating that the language barriers confronting students are actually being overcome, that program may, at that point, no longer constitute appropriate action as far as that school is concerned. We do not believe Congress intended that under § 1703(f) a school would be free to persist in a policy which, although it may have been "appropriate" when adopted, in the sense that there were sound expectations for success and bona fide efforts to make the program work, has, in practice, proved a failure. (p. 1010)

Heavy Runner v. Bremner, 522 F. Supp. 162 (D. Mont. 1981)

Facts and Issues. Claiming violations of the Civil Rights Act of 1964 (42 U.S.C. §2000(d)), the Equal Educational Opportunity Act (20 U.S.C. §1703(f)), and the Fourteenth Amendment, the plaintiffs sought to force the Browning and Heart Butte School Districts to provide all Blackfeet Indian students who are English language deficient with bilingual-bicultural education.

Holding. The court did not grant summary judgment for either of the parties.

Reasoning. Because there was no evidence suggesting the school district denied the students equal educational opportunity, the court ruled that the plaintiffs would have to come to a future trial with proof that the district violated the provisions of the Civil Rights Act of 1964 and the Equal Educational Opportunity Act. Moreover, the court, noting several federal grant applications filed by the school districts, expressed its concern that several language-minority students were burdened in the school district, necessitating the defendants to show at a future time that they were taking appropriate steps to ensure the students' equal participation by overcoming the children's language barriers.

Significance of Ruling. This case philosophically opposed the presumption in *Lau* that the number of affected students being denied remedial language instruction was the basis for seeking relief. Citing *U.S. v. District of Ferndale* (1978) and its accompanying logic, the court found that remedial efforts are required as long as there is at least one person being denied equal educational opportunity. Also, the court reaffirmed what had been found in the *Guadalupe* decision, which stated that language-minority students did not have a constitutional right to a bilingual-bicultural education in the public schools.

Keyes v. *School District No. 1 Denver, Colorado,* 576 F. Supp. 1503 (D. Colo. 1983)

Facts and Issues. Continuing a string of litigation stretching back to 1969, including an appeal in 1975 from a remanded case from the Supreme Court (*Keyes* v. *Denver*, 1973), this court addressed many contentious issues within a complex desegregation plan for Denver School District No. 1. The focus of that litigation was on what had been called the Cardenas Plan, a plan for the bilingual-bicultural education of several Latino students who were limited-English proficient in the Denver School District. The plaintiffs argued that the integration of Latino language-minority students into what had been termed as alien, Anglo schools was a travesty meant to be prohibited by the *Brown* decision in 1954. Effectively, by segregating Latino students through the Cardenas plan, a bilingual-bicultural program, the plaintiffs argued that these same students would finally achieve the opportunity for an equal education required by federal law. The district court agreed and required the inclusion of the Cardenas plan into the desegregation order.

The appeal (*Keyes* v. *Denver*, 1975) was remanded with respect to determining if any relief was necessary to ensure equal educational opportunity for the language-minority children. After the remand, the parties agreed on a desegregation plan. However, that plan, approved in 1976, did not address any of the issues relating to the language-minority students. The plaintiffs' contention in this case was that language-minority children were being denied the opportunity for an equal education because the school system had failed to take appropriate action to address their special needs (*Keyes* v. *Denver*, 1983). This contention was based on the denial of the children's equal protection of the laws guaranteed through mandates and guidelines set forth by the Fourteenth Amendment, the Equal Educational Opportunity Act, and the Civil Rights Act of 1964.

Holding. The court overturned the earlier court's mandate with respect to the inclusion of the Cardenas plan into the desegregation order. The earlier court ruled against all charges of discrimination based on the Fourteenth Amendment and §601 of the Civil Rights Act.

In 1983, the court concluded that the district fell short of providing language-minority students with an effective remedial language program.

Reasoning. In the 1975 decision, the court indicated that no proof supported the claim that plaintiffs had been discriminated against as set forth by the Fourteenth Amendment or §601 of the Civil Rights Act. Furthermore, the court chided the district court for going beyond its limited, remedial role in removing barriers to help language-minority students achieve equal educational opportunity. The court noted that, even if a finding of discrimination were to be found, the earlier decision to adopt the Cardenas Plan went beyond simply helping Latino school children reach the proficiency in English necessary to learn other basic subjects. According to the Supreme Court finding in *San Antonio v. Rodriguez* (1973), education is not considered a fundamental right except for empowering citizens to exercise their right to free speech and voting. In this light, only what is minimally required can be asked of the courts. Instead of merely removing obstacles to effective desegregation, the court's order imposed a comprehensive and intrusive order that actually augmented the segregation of the school district.

In the 1983 decision, the court applied the three-prong *Castañeda* test to assess the district's good-faith effort in providing a remedial language program designed to ensure the equal educational opportunity for language-minority students. The court's conclusion that the district fell short of providing language-minority students with an effective remedial language program was based on the district's lack of assessment protocol for the language program and preliminary evidence suggesting the current program failed to help language-minority students. These facts represent the latter two prongs of the *Castañeda* case. Thus the district was found to have violated 20 U.S.C. §1703 et. seq., otherwise known as the Equal Educational Opportunity Act.

Significance of Ruling. In the 1975 decision, the appeals court ruled that there is no right to a bilingual or bicultural program, even in light of the *Lau* and *Serna* decisions. This court also decided that, with all things considered, desegregation certainly outweighed the bilingual and bicultural needs of language-minority students. The court stated that a bilingual-bicultural program was an option for districts to correct past discrimination in language but was no substitute for solutions addressing desegregation. According to the court, although sound pedagogy may assert the effectiveness of an advanced language program of bilingual education, the Constitution requires only what is minimally effective for language-minority students to achieve equal educational opportunity.

The 1983 case reaffirmed earlier court decisions that ruled any remedial language programs that fail to meet the following criteria are in violation of the Equal Educational Opportunity Act of 1974. The criteria, gleaned from the *Castañeda I* (1981) decision, include: 1) Is the program based on sound education theory or is it, at least, a legitimate experimental strategy? 2) Can the results of the program be evaluated and assessed? and 3) Does the program actually succeed in overcoming the language barriers of language-minority students?

The court further ruled that a failure to take appropriate action to remove language barriers to equal participation in an education program is a failure to establish a unitary school system, thus violating any desegregation mandate. The court referred to an earlier order made in *Keyes* v. *Denver* (1982):

> A unitary school system is one in which all of the students have equal access to the opportunity for education, with the publicly provided educational resources distributed equitably, and with the expectation that all students can acquire a community defined level of knowledge and skills

consistent with their individual efforts and abilities. It provides a chance to develop fully each individual's potentials, without being restricted by an identification with any racial or ethnic groups. (p. 403)

United States v. Board of Education of the City of Chicago, 642 F. Supp. 206 (D. Ill. 1986).

Facts and Issues. Within the frame of an ongoing desegregation case, the U.S. Department of Education (DOE) complained that the Chicago Board of Education (CBE) was improperly using money obtained through a Title VII grant. The problems, according to the DOE, were with the developmental and newcomer bilingual education programs. The purpose of the developmental program was to teach Spanish literacy, as well as Latino culture and history, to language-minority students. The problem, according to the DOE, was that monolingual English-speaking students were also part of the program and that bilingual student tutors, rather than fully certified bilingual teachers, were used to teach these bilingual education programs. The government contended that the relevant statute, 20 U.S.C. §3261, and regulation, 34 C.F.R. §520, forbade spending these federal dollars on teaching Spanish to English-speaking students.

Holding. The court ruled that the district must comply with the DOE requirements regarding the use of student tutors. However, the court also determined that it was acceptable to have a limited number of English-speaking students in the bilingual-bicultural program.

Reasoning. Regarding the developmental program, the court noted that the purpose of the Chicago program was to teach remedial English language skills to Latino students. Just because it also included English-speaking students, the program still met its obligations under Title VII because at least 60% of the students in the bilingual-bicultural literacy program were language-minority students, the minimum number required for compliance.

> In order to prevent the segregation of children on the basis of national origin in programs assisted under this title, and in order to broaden the understanding of children about languages and cultural heritages other than their own . . . a program of bilingual instruction may include the participation of children whose language is English, but in no event shall the percentage of such children exceed 40 per centum. The objective of the program shall be to assist children of limited-English proficiency to improve their English language skills, and the participation of other children in the program must be for the principal purpose of contributing to the achievement of that objective. (20 U.S.C. §3223(a)(4)(B))

The second contention the court faced was the DOE complaint that the Chicago Board's Newcomer Student Program, a bilingual education plan for language-minority students just arriving to the district, improperly used bilingual student tutors to teach a few ethnically diverse students. Student tutors were used because the board contended that it would be economically infeasible, as well as inefficient, to teach the few students of each language who attended the district's schools. However, according to Title VII law at the time, the statute required the district receiving funds to use only the most qualified personnel available, precluding the use of student tutors:

> An application for a grant under this part may be approved only if the Commissioner determines that the program will use the most qualified available personnel, including only those personnel who are proficient in the language of instruction and in English, to the extent possible, and the best resources, and will substantially increase the educational opportunities for children of limited-English proficiency in the area to be served by the applicant. (20 U.S.C. §3223(b)(3)(C)(i))

The DOE further contended that the federal statute related to the provisions in Title VII required language remediation services for all language-minority children in a school district, even if there were only one:

> The term "program of bilingual education" means a program of instruction, designed for children of limited-English proficiency in elementary or secondary schools, in which, with respect to the years of study to which such program is applicable there is instruction given in, and study of, English and, to the extent necessary to allow a child to achieve competence in the English language, the native language of the children of limited-English proficiency, and such instruction is given with appreciation for the cultural heritage of such children, and of other children in American society, and, with respect to elementary and secondary school instruction, such instruction shall, to the extent necessary, be in all courses or subjects of study which will allow a child to progress effectively through the educational system. (20 U.S.C. §3223(a)(4)(A)(i))

The court found no explicit language in the previous statute that required the education of all language-minority students. This argument was rejected: "It is not apparent to us that §3223(a)(4)(A) requires the Board to give bilingual instruction to every LEP child, even one speaking Urdu" (p. 14).

Significance of Ruling. This case illustrates the difficulty districts would face if they had even a few students of multiple ethnicities and language origins. According to the court, Title VII requires all students to receive bilingual instruction by the most qualified individuals, which precludes teacher aides or tutors. However, the court rejected the notion, as *Lau* and *Serna* had, that the district was responsible for just one language-minority student. Interestingly enough, this contradicts the interpretation of 20 U.S.C. §1703 that even if only one language-minority student exists in a district, he or she has the right to a language remediation program., which is a position several courts have taken (*U.S. v. Ferndale*, 1978; *Heavy Runner* v. *Bremner*, 1981). Acceptance of the latter premise poses a dilemma for many districts, which must then educate many different children with limited staff and possibly insufficient resources.

Gomez v. *Illinois State Board of Education,* 811 F.2d 1030 (7th Cir. 1987)

Facts and Issues. Gomez v. *Illinois* (1985) was a class action brought on behalf of the language-minority children enrolled in various local school districts in Illinois. Plaintiffs claimed that their school districts had not tested them for English language proficiency, nor had they received bilingual instruction or remedial instruction. Plaintiffs further asserted that the Illinois State Board of Education and the Illinois State Superintendent of Education had violated Chapter 122, §14C-3 of the Illinois Revised Statutes, which governed transitional bilingual education in the Illinois state school system. The statute required school districts to identify students of limited-English-speaking ability and classify them according to language, grade, age, or achievement level. Any school district with 20 or more students of limited English proficiency must have established a transitional bilingual education program. The Illinois State Board of Education's responsibility under this statute was to develop certain regulations that must be adhered to by the school districts.

Generally, the plaintiffs claimed that the board had violated their rights protected by the Equal Educational Opportunity Act, Title VI of the Civil Rights Act, and the Equal Protection Clause of the Fourteenth Amendment. Specifically, the plaintiffs asked that the defendants be required to provide local school districts with uniform standards for the identification and instruction of language-minority students, even in those districts with fewer than 20 of such students, as well as an appeals process for parents of students placed in language remediation programs.

The 1987 case was an appeal of the 1985 decision, which dismissed all complaints against the school board.

Holding. The circuit court dismissed all of the plaintiffs' motions and directed them to file a new complaint naming local school officials as defendants in the federal district court where the school districts are located.

The circuit court found that the lower court's dismissal of the earlier complaint, concerning the responsible parties for implementing a remedial language program, was improper and would be remanded for further proceedings. However, the court upheld the earlier court's dismissal of the complaints that the board violated the protections under the Equal Educational Opportunity Act and the Civil Rights Act of 1964.

Reasoning. In the 1985 decision, the court found that the board did not, as a policy, intend to discriminate against language-minority students through its uniform standards. The plaintiffs in the 1985 case did not charge the board of education with either past or present purposeful discrimination in attempts to enact its transitional bilingual education programs. Based on this lack of intent to discriminate, the plaintiffs' arguments based on Title VI and the Equal Protection Clause were dismissed. The appeals court affirmed the lower court's ruling.

The 1985 court decided that, since no specific remedy has been set forth in the EEOA for implementing a bilingual education program, the state was free to set up its own program and delegate to local school districts the primary burden of implementing it. Furthermore, once a state has passed a statute setting up a transitional bilingual education program and once the state board of education has drawn up and enacted guidelines for the program's implementation, the burden of implementing the program guidelines shifts to the local school district. This decision did not hold.

Basing its decision on the conclusion of the Ninth Circuit in *Idaho Migrant Council* v. *Board* (1981), the circuit court reasoned that 20 U.S.C. §1703(f) (EEOA) requires that state, as well as local, education agencies ensure that the needs of LEP children are met. Thus the appeals court reversed the earlier district ruling.

Significance of Ruling. This case set forth the requirement that, through the EEOA, the term "education agency" refers to both state and local education agencies, both having the obligation to take "appropriate action to overcome language barriers that impede equal participation by students in instructional programs."

The court went no further than requiring state education agencies to have a certain obligation to remedy these hardships for language-minority students. The level of involvement by the state education agency certainly must be more than delegating all actions required under the EEOA:

> Although the meaning of "appropriate action" may not be immediately apparent without reference to the facts of the individual case, it must mean something more than "no action." State agencies cannot, in the guise of deferring to local conditions, completely delegate in practice their obligations under the EEOA; otherwise, the term "education agency" no longer includes those at the state level. (p. 1042)

Tangipahoa Parish School Board v. *U.S. Department of Education,* 821 F.2d 1022 (5th Cir. 1987)

Facts and Issues. This case involved an appeal by four Louisiana school districts of a U.S. Department of Education's Education Appeals Board decision to require the districts to refund grants made through the Bilingual Education Act (BEA). The districts, namely the parish districts of Tangipahoa, St. John, St. Bernard, and St. Charles, were found in violation of the provision in the BEA that requires a certain percentage of language-minority students to be served through its funded bilingual programs. The districts sought the redress of the courts to challenge the Education Appeals Board's ruling. The focus of this case was the St. Charles Parish School District's acceptance and use of a grant obtained through the BEA.

Holding. The court ruled that the Education Appeals Board correctly concluded that the St. Charles Parish School District violated a provision of the Bilingual Education Act that requires a certain number of qualified students in a bilingual education program to qualify for funding.

Reasoning. With regard to St. Charles Parish, the court ruled that an insufficient number of students actually qualified for the bilingual education programs being funded through the Department of Education. Fewer than 60% of the students qualified through the standardized language-achievement test, with most of the students scoring above the sixth stanine. Also, fewer than 60% of the students in the programs came from families that primarily spoke a language other than English. Another significant finding was that the home-language survey, which is used to identify language-minority students, contained questions that had little to do with qualification standards set forth by the Bilingual Education Act. The court found that the bilingual education programs actually were operated, in most part, as foreign-language programs.

The authority for the Department of Education to recover funds comes from 20 U.S.C. §1234a(e), which states that "a final decision of the [Education Appeals Board] under this section upholding a final audit determination . . . shall establish the amount of the audit determination as a claim of the United States which the State or local educational agency shall be required to pay." The relevant regulation provides that "When a grantee has materially failed to comply with the terms of a grant, [the Department] may suspend the grant, . . . terminate the grant for cause, . . . or take such other remedies as may be legally available and appropriate in the circumstances" (34 C.F.R. §74.1]3(a)).

Significance of Ruling. This ruling indicates that school districts must take care when accepting funds through the Bilingual Education Act. Particular care, as evidenced through this case, should be in the methods used in identifying students for any bilingual education programs funded through Title VII. The court also raised the issue of the actual liability school districts should face if they violate provisions of the BEA. In this case, the court chastised the Department of Education for ordering the districts to refund the Title VII money, money the court says cannot be replaced without taking away from current and future students. This, according to Judge Politz, would be a travesty, hurting innocent children in need of a quality education. However, the court noted the department's justification and right to repayment.

Teresa P. v. Berkeley Unified School District, 724 F. Supp. 698 (N.D. Cal. 1989)

Facts and Issues. Plaintiffs claimed that they had been denied equal educational opportunity due them under the law (the Equal Educational Opportunity Act, 20 U.S.C. §1703(f); §601 of the Civil Rights Act, 42 U.S.C. §2000(d)) because the district failed to take appropriate action to overcome language barriers faced by plaintiffs and to provide them with adequate English language development instruction and adequate instruction and support in their native language. Specifically, the plaintiffs charged that the testing and procedures for the identification and assessment of the district's language-minority students were inadequate and that the district used inappropriate criteria to determine when the district's programs of special language services for individual LEP students were no longer necessary or appropriate. They also claimed that the district failed to allocate adequate resources to the district's special language services for LEP students and had failed to ensure that teachers and other instructional personnel had the requisite qualifications, credentials, and skills to provide these services effectively.

Holding. The court held that the plaintiffs failed to show that the defendants violated the EEOA.

Reasoning. The court stated that the plaintiffs had to show a discriminatory intent on part of the Berkeley Unified School District toward its language-minority students in order to show that the school district violated the Civil Rights Act. According to the court, the plaintiffs failed to do this. The court decided that the district had a program based on sound education theory and that the premise of the program was to increase the achievement of language-minority students, which was achieved according to the standardized test scores, attendance, and classroom grades of these language-minority students. Although mildly criticizing the *Castañeda* test from the Fifth Circuit, the court used it in this case.

The first prong of the *Castañeda* test relies on an assessment of the language program's basis on sound pedagogy or legitimate experimental strategy. The court indicated that its job was not to choose between two competing education theories. Rather, its sole purpose was to assess if the district's strategy attempted to remediate the language barriers in an educationally sound way:

> Given the diversity of opinion in the education field concerning which theoretical and programmatic approach is sound, it is fortunate that this Court is not charged with the difficult task of establishing the ideal program or choosing between competing theories. Instead, this Court is charged solely with the responsibility of determining whether the [district's] program is informed by an educational theory which some experts recognize as sound. (p. 713)

The second prong of the *Castañeda* test is to assess the program's implementation. The plaintiffs argued that the district's use of bilingual tutors did not suffice unless these tutors held a certificate or credential indicating they had the experience and skill to effectively work with language-minority students. The court decided that such credentialing was not needed if a good-faith effort to provide competent teachers was made.

> There is in fact evidence in the record showing that there is no difference in achievement success of LEP students in the [district] between students with credentialed teachers and students who do not have credentialed teachers. (p. 714)

The third prong focuses on the language remediation program's effectiveness. The court saliently presented its qualms in making such a determination:

> Neither the EEOA nor the *Castañeda* court explains how it is that a federal court is to judge the results of a school district's language remediation program. *Castañeda* simply indicated that the program should "produce results indicating that the language barriers confronting students are actually being overcome." 648 F.2d at 1010. Measuring the success or failure of educational programs is one of the great

challenges that faces our educators and is a challenge that this Court approaches with, at least, great trepidation. Other courts have also expressed a similar reluctance. (p. 714)

The *Teresa* court relied on attendance patterns and achievement on California's statewide tests to assess the results of Berkeley's language remediation program, which it found to be compliant and effective.

Significance of Ruling. This case affirmed that, under the Equal Educational Opportunity Act, it is unnecessary for teachers or tutors to be credentialed in a specific language in order to deliver remediation programs to language-minority students as long as the school district makes a good-faith effort to provide competent teachers. Also, it recognized the need of a school district to base any language remediation program on sound pedagogy that results in achievement comparable to non-language-minority students in the same district.

The court noted that it was not required to employ the three-prong *Castañeda* test to ensure that the district's language remediation program was compliant with the EEOA. However, it also noted that it would provide a helpful analytical tool. Not only did this case offer insight into the *Teresa* situation, but it also shed interpretive light on the *Castañeda* guidelines.

People Who Care v. *Rockford Board of Education,* 851 F. Supp. 905 (N.D. Ill. 1993)

Facts and Issues. This case was primarily a lawsuit filed in 1989 to oppose a reorganization plan advanced by the Rockford School District (RSD). In an effort to desegregate the district, the RSD reassigned the bilingual program at various times for desegregation purposes. The court noted that it was discriminatory for the RSD to use language-minority students to comply with desegregation orders and that the RSD persisted in this discrimination even with vocal opposition from the Latino community:

> The transfer of the bilingual students from Barbour and King to Whitehead drew opposition from Hispanic-Ameri-

> can parents concerned about the removal of the program from the heart of the Hispanic community. In December of 1979, the Bilingual Parent Advisory Council (BPAC) initiated a boycott of the Bilingual Program because of transportation problems, frequent relocation of the Program and placing of the program so far away from the Hispanic community so that parents could not easily get to the schools.... Despite a promise to the BPAC (in response to the boycott) that it would attempt to curtail the frequent transfer of the Bilingual Program, the RSD failed to keep its promise. In 1986, Hispanic parents met with Superintendent Mell Grell voicing opposition to the relocation of the bilingual program. The response of the Board was another relocation. (p. 1186)

The court called bilingual education essential for language-minority students and condemned the transfer of the bilingual program from school to school as essentially a mandatory reassignment of the Latino students for desegregation purposes:

> Like the burden placed on African-American students in the RSD, the mandatory reassignment of Hispanic-American students for desegregation purposes was unmatched by the mandatory reassignment of white students for desegregation purposes. (p.1186)

Holding. With respect to the Rockford bilingual education program, the court held that the board violated the constitutional rights of its language-minority students.

Reasoning. Using the three-prong *Castañeda* test, the court decided that the Rockford board not only violated the rights of language-minority students by denying them an effective and meaningful bilingual education program but also unfairly transported them to comply with desegregation efforts. This involuntary transportation, which was carried out with means that were significantly inferior to those used for white students, was not forced on the majority students. Citing *United States* v. *Yonkers Bd. of Education* (1985), this action was expressly forbidden by judicial precedent.

> Further, the school district's transportation policies with respect to specialized programs, such as bilingual education, should not place disproportionate or stigmatizing burdens on minority students. (p. 1192)

Also, because the RSD converted its elementary half-day pull-out bilingual program, which allowed bilingual students to interact with the general school population, into a whole-day program, language-minority students were completely segregated from the rest of the school:

> Further, Bilingual students were steered toward easier and less beneficial classes by English-only speaking counselors and were inadequately provided with educational services and curricula comparable to white students. Furthermore, the RSD failed to adequately identify and assess non- and limited-English-speaking students as eligible to participate in the Bilingual Program. Finally, the RSD failed to provide effective and meaningful special education services to non- and limited-English-speaking students. (p. 1192)

As a result of these practices, the court found that serious deficiencies existed in the RSD bilingual program, and education services received by language-minority students were not equal to those available to students in the regular instructional program. Worse yet, the court noted, the RSD had failed to properly identify and assess students in need of bilingual services. These findings were confirmed by a visit from the Office of Civil Rights:

> To illustrate, on an annual basis, the District determined which students were from non-English-language backgrounds and, thus, potentially non- and limited-English speaking. Principals, classroom teachers and secretaries generally relied on personal knowledge about the student's families to provide this information. In two schools, the Ethnic Code from the Student Information Form was used to identify non-English-language background students, even though ethnicity and home language background are not synonymous. In several other elementary schools, such information was provided by the students themselves or "in conjunction

with students." The OCR considered this last method to be especially inappropriate with elementary-age students who may not have fully understood the questions or the reasons for which the information was sought. Id. The RSD also placed students in nonexistent language groups, for example, "East India, Oriental, Hawaiian, and Indian." (p. 1188)

The OCR found other evidence of district efforts to steer language-minority students to easier classes, which were not in the required college prep curriculum. Other instances of deficiency were noted, such as the lack of bilingual programs where language-minority students went to school, a significant shortage of bilingual mathematics and science books, and history classes limited only to studies of Latin American affairs. The court's opinion was enhanced by a pithy quote from *Cassell* v. *Texas* (1950):

> If one factor is uniform in a continuing series of events that are brought to pass through human intervention, the law would have to have the blindness of indifference rather than the blindness of impartiality not to attribute the uniform factor to man's purpose. The purpose may not be of evil intent or in conscious disregard of what is conceived to be a binding duty. Prohibited conduct may result from misconception of what duty requires. (p. 293)

Significance of Ruling. This case affirmed the precedent set earlier in federal court that a court may consider the school district's conduct relating to bilingual education programs in evaluating the entire school system within the context of a desegregation case. The court relied on an earlier 6th Circuit Court opinion in *Lorain NAACP* v. *Lorain Board* (1991), which found the need to link the continuing success of Lorain's language remediation program to the perceived success of its desegregation efforts. The *Lorain* court came to this conclusion as a result of the previous successes of the Lorain bilingual program in ensuring language-minority student success and reduced dropout rates. Although the *Lorain* and *People Who Care* cases were dissimilar, the *Lorain* case still served as a precedent for allowing desegregation efforts to be judged, to some extent, by the district's efforts in meeting the language remediation needs of its students.

Furthermore, this court affirmed the decisions in *Castañeda* and *Cintron* that the goal of language remediation programs is to integrate Spanish-speaking students into the English language classroom. This is manifested through raising the academic achievement of limited-English-proficient students, thus creating equal educational opportunities for these students. Because of this, language remediation programs should not isolate language-minority students from English-speaking children. Rather, any language remediation program should encourage contact between non-English-speaking and English-speaking children. Allowing participation in mainstream academic and extracurricular programs is one manner of achieving this goal.

Ray M. v. Board of Education, 884 F. Supp. 669 (E.D. N.Y. 1995)

This case was a request for certification as a class for a suit against the school district. The plaintiffs in this case contended that the school district failed to provide them with appropriate and timely special education services as prescribed under state and federal law, particularly with respect to language barriers. Plaintiffs maintained that the defendants had consistently failed to meet their obligations to LEP students and that LEP students typically were placed in what were called alternate interim placements (AIP), which were conducted by monolingual professionals who were not licensed to provide bilingual education. These LEP students would stay in the AIP until a bilingual program was located. The New York State Department of Education determined that LEP students placed in the AIP were not being given an equal education and that their special needs were not being met.

Specifically, the plaintiffs wanted to ensure that the defendant school board provided services and programs recommended in the IEPs and that the services and programs be recommended on the basis of proper evaluations, which would be conducted in the dominant language of the children.

The defendant school district claimed that the courts should not become entangled in determining what type of services LEP students should be given. This court agreed, but it responded that it was not determining what special education services were needed but simply enforcing the district's implementation of those services.

Holding. The court held that the plaintiffs should modify their class request from requiring special education services that meet the student's language needs to only requiring special education services addressed by the IEP and provided by appropriately licensed and trained professionals.

Reasoning. The court reasoned that requiring special education evaluations to be held in the dominant language of the child may redirect the decision-making process away from trained educators to the courts, who should not have that power.

Significance of Ruling. The court openly denounced the mandatory use of bilingual services for special education children while still clarifying the IDEA provision which mandates that states receiving federal funding must develop a plan to provide a free and appropriate education to all children. This includes providing testing and evaluation of students in the child's primary language unless it is not feasible (20 U.S.C. §1412(5)(c)).

OHA v. *DOE*, 951 F. Supp. 1484 (D. Hawaii 1996)

Facts and Issues. The Office of Hawaiian Affairs (OHA) claimed that the Hawaii Department of Education's failure to provide what it deemed to be sufficient use of the Hawaiian language in Hawaii's public schools violated state law as well as the First and Fourteenth Amendments and the Native American Language Act of 1990. The OHA wanted to have the State of Hawaii provide more Hawaiian language immersion programs in public schools because, it concluded, there had been insufficient immersion programs in place. The OHA asked the court to require the Hawaii Department of Education to make Hawaiian language immersion programs more accessible.

Holding. The court decided that the grounds of the case did not merit relief for the plaintiffs, the OHA, within the federal court system. The court remanded all claims not related to §1983 to the state court system.

Reasoning. The court held that because the Native American Language Act (NALA) does not provide for a private cause of action, the plaintiffs would not win a decision against the DOE. NALA, 25 U.S.C. §2903, declares that "it is the policy of the United States to . . . preserve, protect, and promote the rights of Native Americans to use, practice, and develop Native American languages." Moreover, the act provides that the rights of "Native Americans to express themselves through the use of Native American languages shall not be restricted in any public proceeding, including publicly supported education programs" (25 U.S.C. §2904).

The court found that, through the OHA's own admission, the state of Hawaii was not restricting any Hawaiian language programs; the state was simply not providing as many programs as the OHA desired. NALA does not require states to promote a particular language, they are mandated only not to restrict the language of Native Americans. The court ruled that the act speaks in terms of general policy goals and does not create a new set of enforcement regulations.

> NALA consists largely of a statement of "findings" that unique Native American languages and cultures have been suppressed in the past and should now be fostered. Based on these findings NALA sets forth a "declaration of policy" that it is the policy of the United States to encourage and promote the use of Native American languages. 25 U.S.C. §2901, 2903. (p. 1494)

The court continued by asserting that the language of the statute that speaks to the restricting of native languages:

does not place an affirmative duty on states to promote Hawaiian language through funding immersion programs, as suggested by Plaintiffs. Rather, assuming this provision applies to states, at most it prevents the state from barring the use of Hawaiian languages in schools. (p.1494)

Opposite from the OHA contentions, the state actually had been recognized in the enactment of the NALA for its exemplary model of Hawaiian language immersion programs.

One other avenue the OHA pursued was to seek relief through 42 U.S.C. §1983, which essentially sets a three-part test to determine if a statute, which does not have an explicit enforcement mechanism, can be enforced through §1983. The test is:

(1) is the plaintiff an intended beneficiary of the statute, (2) does the statute impose a binding obligation on the state, and (3) is the asserted right too "vague and amorphous" as to be beyond the competence of the judiciary to enforce? (p. 1496)

The court determined that, though the plaintiff was a beneficiary of the state, the statute did not impose a legal obligation on the state to provide for Hawaiian language immersion programs. Also, the ambiguous language of NALA failed to set an explicit enforcement mechanism.

Regarding the challenges based on the First and Fourteenth Amendments, the court stated that the OHA sought retrospective relief based on past discrimination, discrimination that did not exist at the time of the litigation. For this reason, those claims could not be supported by the federal court system, which invokes injunctive decisions in discrimination cases for prospective relief, that is, within the present and future time.

Significance of Ruling. The significance in this case is the court's interpretation of the Native American Language Act of 1990. The court essentially typified this law as a symbolic gesture toward recognizing indigenous languages of the United States, just as one would recognize any language other than English. Because there are no so-called teeth in the law, it cannot be enforced through the federal court system. Even if it could be enforced, the provisions of the act, according to the court, do not call for affirmative actions to be taken with respect to Native American bilingual education.

California Teachers Association v. *Davis,* 64 F. Supp. 2d 945 (C.D. Cal. 1999)

Facts and Issues. This case involved a provision of Proposition 227, titled "English Language in Public Schools," passed by California voters in 1998. The initiative requires non-English-speaking children in California public schools to be taught only in English. This suit challenged only §320, the provision of the initiative that gives parents a private cause of action against teachers and school administrators who violate the law:

> All California school children have the right to be provided with an English language public education. If a California school child has been denied the option of an English language instructional curriculum in public school, the child's parent or legal guardian shall have legal standing to sue for enforcement of the provisions of this statute, and if successful shall be awarded normal and customary attorney's fees and actual damages, but not punitive or consequential damages. Any school board member or other elected official or public school teacher or administrator who willfully and repeatedly refuses to implement the terms of this statute by providing such an English language educational option at an available public school to a California school child may be held personally liable for fees and actual damages by the child's parents or legal guardian. (Cal. Ed. Code §320)

The plaintiffs were individual teachers, teacher organizations, and school administrator organizations who asserted the provision was unconstitutional because the Eleventh Amendment prevents state agencies from being sued, and they sought to enjoin enforcement. The defendants argued that it did not violate the Eleventh

Amendment because the statute's enforcement rests with parents who bring lawsuits against violators of the law. The defendants had lost a preliminary argument regarding jurisdiction.

Since the issue of this case was the potential limitation of free speech, the federal judiciary claimed jurisdiction. The plaintiffs' complaint, which was then allowed to be heard, asserted that the law was overbroad and vague and thus violated the First and Fourteenth Amendments.

Holding. The court rejected the plaintiffs' claims and ruled in favor of the state and its related defendants.

Reasoning. Because the proposition does not completely prohibit languages other than English used in disciplining students, emergency training, social interactions, tutoring, or parent-teacher conferences, teachers' free speech rights are not abridged in any way. Although teachers are afforded some First Amendment rights in situations outside the curriculum, the proposition does not prohibit languages other than English in these situations. The proposition involves a policy decision on curriculum, in which teachers are required to hold lessons for English learners in English, rather than in their native language. The court concluded that teachers do not have a First Amendment right to be free of regulations that tell them to follow a method of instruction or a curriculum. Citing *Bishop* v. *Aronov* (1991), the court reasserted the state's right to regulate in-class speech as long as it relates to legitimate education goals.

The challenges that the proposition was ambiguously and vaguely worded also did not hold merit in the court's reasoning because the proposition clearly requires English to be the only official language of instruction.

In the Fourteenth Amendment challenge regarding due process for teachers and administrators sued in the name of Proposition 227, the court rejected the need for any special safeguards, because the statute leaves teachers in the same position as that of all other potential litigants, who are free to defend themselves against similarly trivial or non-meritorious lawsuits.

Significance of Ruling. The court distinctly separated when school officials must use English only and when they are not required to do so. Proposition 227 requires school officials to use English only in instruction and the direct education of its students. Other situations, such as disciplining students and communicating with parents, appear to enjoy more latitude with respect to the language being spoken.

Valeria v. Wilson, 307 F.3d 1036

Facts and Issues. On 2 June 1998 California voters, by a 61% majority, approved Proposition 227, an initiative titled "English Language in Public Schools" and codified as "English Language Education for Immigrant Children." The statute amended the California Education Code (§300 et. seq.) to change the system under which students who are limited in English proficiency are educated in California's public schools. Specifically, Proposition 227 was based on the idea that:

> The public schools of California currently do a poor job of educating immigrant children, wasting financial resources on costly experimental language programs whose failure over the past two decades is demonstrated by the current high drop-out rates and low English-literacy levels of many immigrant children. (§300 (d))

Also, §300 (a) and (b) state that:

> The English language is the national public language of the United States of America and of the state of California, is spoken by the vast majority of California residents, and is also the leading world language for science, technology, and international business, thereby being the language of opportunity; and . . . [allows immigrant children] to fully participate in the American dream of economic and social advancement.

Proposition 227 requires limited-English-proficient (LEP) children to receive instruction through what is called *sheltered English immersion* or *structured English immersion.* In other words, children will be taught English during a temporary transition period not normally intended to exceed one year. According to §305 of Proposition 227, "Once English learners have acquired a good working knowledge of English, they shall be transferred to English language mainstream classrooms." Certain children, specified in §311, may be granted a parental exception waiver to this requirement. These children include those who already know English, those who are ten years or older, and those with "special physical, emotional, psychological, or educational needs" who have tried the immersion program for 30 days. Also, the school must agree that an alternative course of study would better suit the student's development. However, the initiative does not preclude the occasional use of an LEP student's primary language in or outside the classroom, such as with tutors or teacher's aides. The initiative also does not prohibit additional primary language assistance after an LEP child transitions into a mainstream classroom.

Several civil rights organizations challenged the constitutionality of Proposition 227 one day after it was passed by the people of California. The plaintiffs in this case moved for a preliminary injunction to prevent the implementation of Proposition 227 pending the trial of this case. Defendants Governor Pete Wilson, the State Board of Education, and the State Superintendent of Public Instruction opposed the motion.

Holding. Northern Federal District Court Judge Charles Legge ruled in favor of the initiative, and his opinion was affirmed by the Ninth Circuit Federal Court of Appeals.

Reasoning. The plaintiffs, who asked for an injunction against the implementation of Proposition 227, asked the court to decide that the newly adopted statute could not be considered an "appropriate action" under §1703 of the EEOA. First, the plaintiffs, with the help of expert witnesses, attempted to show that Proposition 227 was based on an unsound education theory. However, advocates of Proposition 227 presented evidence that the sheltered English immersion program of Proposition 227 is based on a sound education theory, "which is not only tested but is the predominant method of teaching immigrant children in many countries in Western Europe, Canada, and Israel" (p. 1018). Therefore, the court concluded that the English immersion system was a valid education theory, thus satisfying the first prong of the *Castañeda* test.

Plaintiffs also argued that the bilingual education program proposed by Proposition 227 has no method by which to assess students' individual needs or evaluate students' individual progress. However, the court stated that there is nothing in the statute that "precludes the State Board of Education from requiring, or local school districts from implementing, adequate methods or individual assessment and evaluation" (p. 1020). Therefore the court decided that is unlikely that there is "no set of circumstances under which California's schools can adopt programs reasonably calculated to implement the educational theory of Proposition 227" (p.1020).

Regarding the third prong of the *Castañeda* case, there was no way to evaluate any results because Proposition 227 had just been implemented, and there was no prima facie evidence to suggest that the results would be damaging to students or that the program would not be able to be later re-evaluated and modified.

Plaintiffs in this case also argued that Proposition 227 violated Title VI of the Civil Rights Act of 1964 because "it imposes an unjustifiable disparate impact on national origin minorities by denying LEP students meaningful access to academic curriculum during its sheltered English immersion program, and then shunting them prematurely into mainstream academic classrooms" (p. 1022). Even though the Supreme Court held in *Washington* v. *Davis* (1976) that a discriminatory purpose, and not simply a disparate impact or effect, must be shown to establish a violation of the Equal Protection Clause, this court, along with the Ninth Circuit, took the position that:

> Where a lawsuit is brought to enforce the regulations under Title VI, rather than the statute itself, and where the plaintiffs seek injunctive or declaratory relief as opposed to compensatory relief, plaintiffs can prove a Title VI violation by establishing only a discriminatory effect. (p. 1023)

However, according to Judge Legge, the defendants in the *Valeria* case did not seem to intentionally discriminate against LEP students. Therefore, the court reasoned, there was no evidence of discriminatory intent, nor would there be an adverse effect, exclusion, denial of benefits, or discrimination.

Finally, the opponents of Proposition 227 argued that the statute violated the Equal Protection Clause of the Fourteenth Amendment by denying them the equal opportunity to secure future legislation for programs that will benefit them, because Proposition 227 can be amended only by the electorate or by a statute approved by a two-thirds vote in each house of the legislature and signed by the governor. The court rejected the idea that the plaintiffs are unduly burdened by the passage of Proposition 227. Options included a statewide initiative campaign to repeal Proposition 227, and opportunities existed for opponents of the statute to petition local school boards for regulations dealing with the implementation of Proposition 227 and its exceptions. Therefore the plaintiffs were not denied equal protection, because they had remedies that they could have sought if they so wished.

In this case, the court stated that there is no constitutional right to bilingual education, as shown in the case of *Guadalupe Organization Inc. v. Tempe Elementary School District* (1978). Also, the court ruled that the Bilingual Education Act could not serve as a basis for a Supremacy Clause challenge to the state statute because, though the Bilingual Education Act actively encourages bilingual education, it cannot require it under 20 U.S.C. §7401 et. seq.

Significance of Ruling. This case reaffirmed the position taken in the *Castañeda* and *Gomez* cases and forcefully asserted the absence of any right to a bilingual education. Rather, the court insisted that the measure was the will of the people and should be given a chance to supplant any belief that bilingual education is the only way to educate language-minority children. This case also continued the practice of applying the *Castañeda* three-prong test in determining if a language-remediation program constituted appropriate action.

CHAPTER FOUR

Legislation and Statutes

Fourteenth Amendment

The cornerstone of all civil rights legislation, the Fourteenth Amendment guarantees to protect individuals from arbitrary or unreasonable state action impairing life, liberty, or property interests. The Fourteenth Amendment to the United States Constitution states:

> No State shall make or enforce any law which shall abridge the privileges or immunities of citizens of the United States, nor shall any state deprive any person of life, liberty, or property, without due process of law; nor deny to any person within its jurisdiction the equal protection of the laws.

This constitutional mandate has become a cornerstone in the protection of civil rights and equal educational opportunity for public school students.

Title VI of the Civil Rights Act of 1964

The Civil Rights Act of 1964 has been a significant part of the language policy issue, banning all forms of discrimination on the grounds of race, color, or national origin in any federally funded program. The statute states, in part:

> No person in the United States shall, on the ground of race, color, or national origin, be excluded from participation in, be denied the benefits of, or be subjected to discrim-

ination under any program or activity receiving Federal financial assistance. (42 U.S.C. §2000(d))

The accompanying regulation, specific to the Department of Education, echoes the wording of 42 U.S.C. §2000(d)) and prohibits discrimination specific to education programs:

> No person in the United States shall, on the ground of race, color, or national origin be excluded from participation in, be denied the benefits of, or be otherwise subjected to discrimination under any program to which this part applies. (34 C.F.R. §100.3)

The Supreme Court decided in *Lau* that the San Francisco Unified School District had the responsibility to instruct students in English because of an applicable requirement by the predecessor to the current Department of Education, the U.S. Department of Health, Education and Welfare. The guideline stated that:

> Where inability to speak and understand the English language excludes national-origin minority group children from effectively participating in the educational program offered by a school district, the district must take affirmative steps to rectify the language deficiency in order to open its instructional program to these students. (35 Fed. Reg. 11595)

This regulation has become better known as the May 1970 Memorandum, a clarification of the guidelines related to the Civil Rights Act of 1964.

Equal Educational Opportunity Act of 1974

The Equal Educational Opportunity Act of 1974 requires appropriate action by a school district in overcoming language barriers that impede a student's equal participation in the education process. The law states:

> No State shall deny equal educational opportunity to an individual on account of his or her race, color, sex, or national origin, by the failure by an educational agency to take

appropriate action to overcome language barriers that impede equal participation by its students in its instructional programs. (20 U.S.C. §1703(f))

This statute has become a standard in establishing language remediation programs in the United States, particularly with the decision in *Castañeda* v. *Pickard* (1981), which established specific criteria for determining if a language remediation program constituted what the statute calls "appropriate action." However, the Office of Civil Rights, the primary enforcer of language-minority rights under Title VI, actively uses the *Castañeda* guidelines, thus ensuring "appropriate action" under the EEOA requirements.

Native American Language Act of 1990

The Native American Language Act of 1990 addresses the right of Native Americans to express themselves through the use of Native American languages without restriction "in any public proceeding, including publicly supported education programs" (25 U.S.C. §2903). Exactly how this law will affect the future of language remediation programs, particularly those with an English-only focus, is not yet known. However, the act does mention in §2906 that the use of English will not be prohibited in the teaching of Indian students. One case is known to have addressed this issue (*OHA* v. *DOE*, 1996).

Individuals with Disabilities Education Act of 1997

The Individuals with Disabilities Education Act (IDEA) requires education agencies to accommodate the needs of disabled students or parents of disabled students who speak a language other than English. Specifically, IDEA requires that local education agencies take into account the language needs of limited-English-proficient children as pertaining to their individualized education plans. In addition, evaluation materials used to assess a child's ability or disability must be administered in the child's native tongue and used on a nondiscriminatory basis; that is, psychological and achievement tests cannot be racially or culturally biased. Federal law also gives parents of such children a right to have all notifications of referrals and evaluations communicated in their native language (20 U.S.C. §1414 et. seq.).

Title III of the No Child Left Behind Act of 2001

The English Language Proficiency and Academic Achievement Act (Title III of the No Child Left Behind Act of 2001) consolidated the Bilingual Education Act with the Emergency Immigrant Education Program, transforming previous law to focus existing programs on teaching English to limited-English-proficient children, including immigrant children and youth, and expediting their transition to mainstream education classes.

Besides renaming the Office of Bilingual Education and Minority Languages Affairs as the Office of Educational Services for Limited English Proficient Children, Title III of the No Child Left Behind Act of 2001 has drastically changed the provisions of grants serving limited-English-proficient students. In general, states will have more chances to obtain and use grant money to educate limited-English-proficient students but will have lost the opportunity to use a student's native language beyond three years.

According to Congress, the primary goals of Title III are to increase the knowledge and use of English among limited-English-proficient children, to increase graduation rates among limited-English-proficient children, and to prepare students for transition as soon as possible into classrooms where instruction is not tailored for limited-English-proficient children.

States now can request grant money to provide assistance to limited-English-proficient children using English, not just the native language of the student. In the spirit of spending more money at the local level, states must distribute at least 95% of their block grants to eligible education agencies to provide assistance to limited-English-proficient children. However, eligible entities are able to choose the method of instruction they would use to teach these children. Title III eliminates the previous requirement that 75% of funding be used to support programs using a child's native language for instruction. To ensure a fair distribution of grant money, small states are guaranteed at least $500,000 under the grant program formula. An additional guarantee is that the allotment of funds will not be affected by the method of instruction employed in the language remediation programs in use in the state. Title III grants are awarded according to a formula based 80% on the number of limited-English-proficient children in the state and 20% on the number of immigrant children and youth in the state. This information is taken from the U.S. Census for the first two years. After this time, the data will come from the number of students being assessed for English proficiency in a state or data from the American Community Survey, which is available from the Department of Commerce, whichever the Department of Education determines to be the most accurate.

States must develop, and will be held accountable for, annual, measurable, achievement objectives to monitor the progress of LEP students in attaining English proficiency. Furthermore, school districts are required to notify parents of a program's failure to meet such achievement objectives for two years. After four years of failing to meet the achievement objectives, the state must require the school district to restructure its curriculum, program, and method of instruction. Specifically, Title III requires school districts receiving grant awards to complete an evaluation every year on the progress students are making toward learning English and achieving the same high levels of academic achievement as other students.

Title III Guidelines. For a Title III grant, the state education agency must agree to certain guidelines. The state education agency must:

- Monitor the progress of students enrolled in programs and activities receiving assistance in attaining English proficiency and in meeting challenging academic achievement standards.

- Establish standards and benchmarks for English language development that are aligned with the state's academic content and achievement standards.
- Ensure that eligible school districts annually test the English proficiency of children who have been in the United States for three or more consecutive years.
- Develop high-quality annual assessments to measure English language proficiency and require school districts to assess the English proficiency of all children with limited-English-proficiency.
- Develop increasingly challenging annual performance objectives for raising the level of English proficiency in reading, writing, speaking, and listening comprehension of each limited-English-proficient student.
- Require school districts to structure their language remediation programs so that they do not rely on continued federal support.
- Reserve 75% of Title III subgrants for school districts with at least 500 LEP students or 3% of the district's total enrollment, whichever is less.
- Reserve the other 25% of Title III subgrants for school districts that have experienced significant increases, as compared to the previous 2 years, in the percentage or number of children and youth with limited-English-proficiency, including recent immigrant children that have enrolled in its schools.

Furthermore, school districts that receive Title III funds must:

- Ensure that their language remediation programs will enable children to speak, read, write, and comprehend the English language and meet challenging state academic content standards and challenging state student academic achievement standards.
- Use qualified personnel who are proficient in English and who have appropriate training and professional credentials in teaching English to LEP children.
- Annually assess the English proficiency of all LEP children participating in programs.

- Base their language remediation programs on sound reading research and sound research and theory on teaching limited-English-proficient children.
- Explain how students enrolled in the programs and activities proposed in the application will be proficient in English after three academic years of enrollment.
- Not be in violation of any state law, including state constitutional law, regarding the education of limited-English-proficient children.

Title III-Approved Activities. Schools can use Title III grants for any of the following activities that contribute to improving limited-English-proficient students' knowledge and use of English:

- Developing and implementing elementary or secondary school English language instructional programs that are coordinated with other relevant programs and services.
- Upgrading program objectives and implementing effective instructional strategies for the language remediation program.
- Acquiring and upgrading curricula, instructional materials, education software, and assessment procedures for the language remediation program.
- Providing academic and vocational education services, as well as tutoring programs that provide early intervention and intensive instruction, for limited-English-proficient children.
- Providing professional development to classroom teachers, principals, administrators, and other school or community-based organizational personnel to improve the instruction and assessment of limited-English-proficient students.
- Acquiring or developing education technology or instructional materials; providing access to and participation in electronic networks for materials, training, and communications; and incorporating such resources in curricula and programs in order to improve the instruction of limited-English-proficient children.
- Providing family literacy services and parent outreach and training activities to limited-English-proficient children and

their families to improve their English language skills and assist parents in helping their children to improve their academic performance.

Testing. Assessments of limited-English-proficient children participating in Title III-funded programs can be in the student's native language if that will give the most accurate and reliable information on what students know and can do in the tested content areas. However, an assessment of reading or language arts skills of any student who has attended school in the United States (excluding Puerto Rico) for three or more consecutive school years must be in English. The school district may, on a case-by-case basis and for only one additional year, use assessments in the child's native language if it would represent a more accurate and reliable evaluation on what the student knows and can do.

Parental Consent and Outreach. School districts are required to inform parents why their child is in need of placement in a language remediation program. Parents have the right to choose among instruction programs if more than one type of program is offered, and they have the right to remove their child from a program for LEP children. Title III also requires school districts to implement effective means of parental outreach to encourage parents to become informed and active participants in their child's language education.

Specifically, parent outreach should include:

- Explaining the reasons that students have been identified as being in need of English language instruction.
- Informing the parents of the child's level of English proficiency, how the level was assessed, and the status of the child's academic achievement.
- Explaining how the language remediation program will specifically help the child acquire English and meet age-appropriate standards for grade promotion and graduation, and what the specific exit requirements are for the program.

- Detailing the expected rate of transition from the language remediation program into a classroom that is not tailored for limited-English-proficient children.
- Informing parents of the expected rate of graduation from high school (if applicable).

Other Title III Considerations. The English Language Proficiency and Academic Achievement Act specifically warns districts and state education agencies not to admit or exclude students from any federally assisted education program, notably Title III, on the basis of a surname or language-minority status.

Programs authorized and funded under Title III that serve Native American children, Native Pacific Island children, and children in Puerto Rico may include programs of instruction, teacher training, curriculum development, evaluation, and testing designed for Native American children learning and studying Native American languages and Puerto Rican children learning and studying Spanish. However, a primary goal of these programs must be focused on increased English proficiency.

CHAPTER FIVE

Trends and Implications

The legal trends discussed in this chapter are based on the doctrine of judicial precedent. U.S. courts tend to follow the principle of *stare decisis*, which essentially means that courts "should decide similar cases in the same way unless there is a good reason for the court to do otherwise" (Statsky and Wernet 1995, p. 7). Thus judicial precedents serve as reasonable and reliable guides for making decisions. It is important to remember that, because the U.S. court system is hierarchical, rulings of the higher courts always take precedence. Furthermore, court decisions in one circuit are not binding in courts of other circuits. However, because many judicial precedents have been noted among the circuits in this study, many principles and precedents can be generalized and applied to future cases.

The federal court system is made up of 12 circuits comprising 94 districts. The following list outlines the geographic breakdown of each circuit:

First Circuit: Maine, Massachusetts, New Hampshire, Rhode Island, and Puerto Rico.
Second Circuit: Connecticut, New York, Vermont.
Third Circuit: Delaware, New Jersey, Pennsylvania, Virgin Islands.
Fourth Circuit: Maryland, North Carolina, South Carolina, Virginia, West Virginia.
Fifth Circuit: Louisiana Mississippi, Texas.
Sixth Circuit: Kentucky, Michigan, Ohio, Tennessee.
Seventh Circuit: Illinois, Indiana, Wisconsin.

Eighth Circuit: Arkansas, Iowa, Minnesota, Nebraska, North Dakota, South Dakota.
Ninth Circuit: Alaska, Arizona, California, Guam, Hawaii, Idaho, Montana, Nevada, Northern Mariana Islands, Oregon, Washington.
Tenth Circuit: Colorado, Kansas, New Mexico, Oklahoma, Utah, Wyoming.
Eleventh Circuit: Alabama, Florida, Georgia.
District of Columbia Circuit.

The Supreme Court laid the foundation for current law with *Lau* v. *Nichols* (1974), which stressed every school district's obligation to abide by §601 of the Civil Rights Act and the then-HEW guidelines. It also provided the basis for proving civil rights and equal education opportunity discrimination, that is, discriminatory effect, under §601 of the Civil Rights Act (42 U.S.C. §2000(d)). Discriminatory effect was hotly debated in the following decades.

By a large margin, the Fifth and Ninth Circuit courts each heard the most cases related to language policy matters in public education. This is no surprise, because the three states with the largest percentage of language-minority students, Texas, New Mexico, and California, reside within these two circuits. Both circuits seem to share a common idea of what the government is required to provide for language-minority students and what constitutes discrimination under §601 of the Civil Rights Act of 1964 or the Equal Protection Clause of the Fourteenth Amendment.

Fifth Circuit Court Cases

In the 1970s the courts in the Fifth Circuit did not have much interest in becoming involved in language remediation policies, as evidenced by its decisions in *Arvizu* v. *Waco ISD* (1973) and *Alvarado* v. *El Paso ISD* (1976). While the courts voiced their general support for Mexican-American children who had language deficiencies, they denied them significant support or relief from the denial of educational opportunity. Although the district court in *Morales* v. *Turman* mandated bilingual education and culturally neutral tests for Latino student-inmates in 1974, the court merely based its decision on expert testimony and not federal law or judicial precedent.

This began to change with the *In re Alien* (1980), which chastised the Texas government for denying language-remediation services to undocumented alien children. However, the district did not fully embrace the idea of bilingual education as the way to comply with §1703 of the Equal Educational Opportunity Act.

Although the *United States* v. *Texas* decision in 1981 fully supported the use of bilingual education, such programs were deemed necessary only to transition language-minority children into mainstream English-speaking classrooms. The *Texas* decision also stressed the need to evaluate compliance with the EEOA on a school district by school district basis. One other salient point of this decision is that it cited *Washington* v. *Davis* (1976) in order to require plaintiffs to show discriminatory intent, rather than simply a disparate impact or effect, in order to prove a violation of §601 of the Civil Rights Act of 1964. This decision placed a heavier burden on plaintiffs in civil rights discrimination cases.

Perhaps the most significant contribution of the Fifth Circuit was the decision in *Castañeda* v. *Pickard* (1981) that bilingual education is not required under 20 U.S.C. §1703(f). The three-prong *Castañeda* test has become the defining standard of compliance for the Equal Educational Opportunities Clause (20 U.S.C. §1703(f)), and it has been used by many of the federal and state judicial districts.

Ninth Circuit Court Cases

The earliest federal case in the Ninth Circuit was *Guadalupe* v. *Tempe* (1978), in which the court criticized the Tenth Circuit opinion in *Serna* (1974) and outraged bilingual education advocates by asserting the decision in *San Antonio* (1973) that there is no fundamental right to a public education, much less a bilingual-bicultural education. It asserted that the Fourteenth Amendment requires only what is minimally effective to overcome language barriers and nothing more. This decision has been supported by the related Ninth Circuit cases *Heavy Runner* v. *Bremner* (1981) and *Valeria* v. *Wilson* (1998).

Interestingly, the *Heavy Runner* case, without making an affirmative judgment for the plaintiff, supported Sixth and Eighth Circuit precedents by requiring equal educational opportunity for all language-minority students, even if there is only one such student in the school district (*United States* v. *School District of Ferndale*, 1978; *Deerfield* v. *Ipswich*, 1979). The judicial basis for this decision is the language of 20 U.S.C. §1703(f), which specifically refers to an individual as one whose rights cannot be breached. This explains the stark contrast to the decisions in *Lau* and *Serna* that gave merit only to claims by a number of disadvantaged children. The difference is that both *Lau* and *Serna* made their rulings based on §601 of the Civil Rights Act of 1964 (42 U.S.C. §2000(d)), rather than the Equal Educational Opportunities Clause.

Other Ninth Circuit opinions shed interpretive light on §1703 of the Equal Educational Opportunity Act and §601 of the Civil Rights Act of 1964. The court in *Idaho Migrant Council* v. *Board* (1981) ruled that, under both statutes, both state and local education agencies shared responsibility for implementing an effective language-remediation program designed to overcome language barriers. Also, a school district establishing a bilingual program under the auspices of the Equal Educational Opportunity Act must make a good-faith effort to provide competent teachers for such a program. But the act does not require teachers or tutors in a language-remediation program to hold specific certificates or credentials (*Teresa* v. *Berkeley*, 1989).

Proposition 227, which restructured the California education system to replace bilingual education with what is called "structured English immersion," has been a substantial issue before the Ninth Circuit. Various motions and orders against the proposition have made it to the federal courts, even one day after the initiative's passage.

The first challenge to Proposition 227 was through *Valeria* v. *Wilson* (1998). The Ninth Circuit refused to enjoin the implementation of the statute for a number of reasons. First, it stated that because the measure was passed by a substantial number (60%) of the people of California, the change seemed to be the explicit will of the people. Second, the due-process requirements of the Fourteenth Amendment were not violated because there existed ample opportunities to oppose the measure and there remains the option to seek repeal of the law. Third, the court decided that the measure did not violate federal law because judicial precedent was that no right to a bilingual education exists. The Bilingual Education Act (Title VII of the IASA) merely encourages bilingual education; it cannot require it. Invoking what has become the standard for judging a language remediation program's compliance under §1703 of the Equal Educational Opportunity Act, the court judged the merits of the state's plan against the three-prong *Castañeda* test, and the program met all three requirements. Finally, the charge that Proposition 227 violated §601 of the Civil Rights Act of 1964 was found lacking. Of prominent note was the court's interpretation of the much debated issue of whether discriminatory intent or simply a discriminatory effect is required to prove a violation of §601. It stated that a §601 violation can exist through the less demanding proof of discriminatory effect if the plaintiffs seek only injunctive relief to enforce Title VI regulations.

The Ninth Circuit also had to make an additional ruling related to Proposition 227. In *California Teachers Association* v. *Davis* (1999), various California educators feared that the language of Proposition 227 prevented them from using any foreign language in the business of the school, which would be tantamount to a violation of their First Amendment rights. This was found to not be the case. The measure and the related statute prohibit foreign languages only in the direct instruction of public school students. The court clarified that educators could still use foreign languages to communicate with parents and students in noninstructional situations.

Other Circuit Court Cases

The Second Circuit has shown distinct support of bilingual education programs since the 1970s. The *Aspira* decree and its affirmation through *Rios* v. *Read* (1978) was echoed by the *Cintron* court's decision on what is an effective bilingual education program. Not until 1995 was a district court in the Second District given another chance to offer an opinion on language policy matters in education. The court in *Ray* v. *Board* (1995) had that opportunity and politely refused.

The Third, Sixth, and Eight Circuit Courts voiced a major opinion or made a significant decision in only one case each. However, each of those cases gives significant insight into public education language policy. The *Evans* v. *Buchanan* (1981) decision restated other circuits' opinion that the federal court system should not have to address the issue of bilingual education, especially within the context of a desegregation case; that is, such matters are best left to state and local education agencies.

A case from Michigan, *Martin Luther King Jr. Elementary School Children* v. *Ann Arbor School District* (1979), extended the idea of language barriers beyond foreign languages to include dialects of English. Black children in the Ann Arbor School District had difficulty learning standard English because they spoke Ebonics, a form of black English. The district court ruled that this language barrier must be overcome by virtue of §1703 to ensure that all children in that district had an equal educational opportunity. The court ordered, among other things, that teachers must take into account the home language of such students when teaching standard English.

In what could have been a test pitting the importance of religious freedom against that of language rights, the decision in *Deerfield* v. *Ipswich* (1979) clearly delineated the state's responsibility to provide equal educational opportunity but rejected the notion that a religious community has the right to a school and bilingual education program of its own. Basing its decision on the Fourteenth Amendment and the Equal Educational Opportunity

Act, the court in *Deerfield* found that there is no constitutional or any other federal right to a bilingual education program, much less an entire school to serve a religious community simply because that community speaks a language other than English.

In *Armstrong* v. *O'Connell* (1977) the Seventh Circuit affirmed one of the Fifth Circuit's more salient decisions: Desegregation solutions cannot be made at the expense of a third ethnic-minority class (*United States* v. *Texas*, 1972). According to this holding, language-remediation programs in the Fifth and Seventh Circuits could not be limited or abandoned to make a desegregation plan work. The logic was that such a denial of equal educational opportunity should not be endured by any class of student.

This protection of language-minority students was further extended in the Seventh Circuit by the detailed holding in *People Who Care* v. *Rockford* (1993), which stressed that the transportation of language-remediation or bilingual education students should not burden or stigmatize minority children. This placed a limit on the measures a school district can take to modify language-remediation programs within a desegregation case. All such matters are important, according to the *People* court, for judicial precedent from the Sixth Circuit has established that a school district's conduct regarding language remediation programs can be used to evaluate the entire school district in a desegregation case (*Lorain NAACP* v. *Lorain Board*, 1991).

Particular care has to be taken when a school district accepts federal funding for bilingual education programs. That was especially true with funds authorized by Title VII of the Elementary and Secondary Education Act. The decision in *United States* v. *Chicago School Board* (1986) detailed the specific requirements that Title VII, commonly known as the Bilingual Education Act, held for federally funded language-remediation programs. However, those rules have changed with the adoption of Title III of the No Child Left Behind Act of 2001. Title III revamps the process to include language remediation programs using English language instruction and not just bilingual instruction.

The Seventh Circuit stand on the Equal Educational Opportunity Act cannot be overemphasized. Significantly, both *Gomez* and *People*, offering only mild criticism of the guidelines, used the three-pronged *Castañeda* test from the Fifth Circuit to determine if the language remediation programs in their cases were compliant with §1703 of the Equal Educational Opportunity Act. This indicates a more universal acceptance of the test as the standard for judging §1703 compliance.

The Tenth Circuit offers a distinct contrast within its own jurisdiction. Although the *Serna* (1974) court decided that language-minority children had the right to a bilingual-bicultural program because of discrimination under §601 of the Civil Rights Act of 1964, the same court ruled in *Keyes* (1975) that no right to a bilingual education program exists. This holding was continued in the *Otero* case, which indicated its opposition to a court imposing such a program on a school district. The basis for this was the opinion in *San Antonio* v. *Rodriguez* (1973) which indicated that there is no fundamental right to an education beyond what is minimally needed to participate in the political process. Although *Serna* and *Otero* differed on the constitutional right to a bilingual education, both echoed Judge Blackmun's opinion in *Lau* that a finding of discrimination should be considered in light of the number of children affected by the alleged discrimination.

The Tenth Circuit also must be singled out for being the first federal court to adopt the three-prong *Castañeda* test advanced by the Fifth Circuit Court of Appeals. Using these guidelines, the Tenth Circuit affirmed another district's method for determining what language remediation programs constitute "appropriate action," as required by 20 U.S.C. §1703(f) (EEOA).

Federal Statutes and Regulations

Various laws, regulations, and informal rules have shaped how language-minority students are to be treated, especially with respect to their language remediation needs. The equal educational opportunity provision in 20 U.S.C. §1703 et. seq. is not the only law that addresses the needs of language-minority students.

The Native American Language Act of 1992 addresses the right of Native Americans to express themselves through the use of Native American languages without restriction "in any public proceeding, including publicly supported education programs" (25 U.S.C. §2903). Exactly how this law will affect the future of language remediation programs, particularly those with an English-only focus, is yet to be known. However, the act does mention in §2906 that the use of English will not be prohibited in the teaching of Native American students. One case is known to have addressed this issue: *OHA* v. *DOE* (1996).

The Individuals with Disabilities Education Act (IDEA) also requires education agencies to accommodate the needs of disabled students or parents of disabled students who speak a language other than English. Specifically, the IDEA requires that local education agencies take into account the language needs of limited-English-proficient children when writing their individualized education plans (IEP). In addition, evaluation materials used to assess a child's ability or disability must be administered in the child's native tongue and used on a nondiscriminatory basis; that is, psychological and achievement tests cannot be racially or culturally biased. Federal law also gives parents of such children a right to have all notifications of referrals and evaluations communicated in their native language (20 U.S.C. §1414 et. seq.).

Although the Equal Educational Opportunity Act has become the primary justification for addressing the needs of language-minority students, Title VI of the Civil Rights Act still carries considerable weight, as evidenced in *Lau* and related decisions. The Office for Civil Rights (OCR) within the Department of Education has the primary responsibility for ensuring that school districts receiving federal funds comply with Title VI and other nondiscrimination statutes.

The May Memorandum, a crucial piece in the *Lau* decision, is the foundation for the OCR's authority to evaluate compliance with Title VI. This memorandum has been an unofficial but widely accepted guideline for interpreting how Title VI applies to education programs for language-minority students. Strengthened by the Supreme Court's affirmation of the memorandum in *Lau*, the

OCR updated the May Memorandum in 1985 and 1991, detailing the procedures for determining whether a school district is taking affirmative steps to make a language remediation program accessible to language-minority students.

The two general guidelines the OCR currently employs for determining Title VI compliance are: 1) determining if there is a need for a language remediation program, and 2) determining if the alternative language program is an adequate vehicle for addressing the needs of language-minority students. To determine if the latter condition has been met, the OCR uses the widely accepted *Castañeda* test. The OCR viewed the *Castañeda* standard as an acceptable test because of the striking similarity between the EEOA and the policy established in the May Memorandum of 1970. The 1991 memorandum, titled "Policy Update on School's Obligations Toward National Origin Minority Students with Limited-English Proficiency (LEP Students)," noted that any remedy that satisfied the EEOA under 20 U.S.C. §1703(f) satisfied the requirements of Title VI.

The OCR elaborated on these guidelines in its public statement, "The Provision of an Equal Education Opportunity to Limited-English Proficient Students," revised in August 2000 and available on the Office of Civil Rights website (www.ed.gov/offices/OCR/). Within the statement, the OCR presented what it considers to be important issues in special language services:

1. Has the school district identified all LEP students who need special language assistance?
2. Can the district ensure the placement of LEP students in appropriate programs?
3. Are all LEP students who need a special language-assistance program being provided such a program?
4. Has the district taken steps to modify a program for LEP students when that program is not working?
5. Has the district ensured that LEP students are not misidentified as students with disabilities because of their inability to speak and understand English?

6. Has the district ensured that parents who are not proficient in English are provided with appropriate and sufficient information about all school activities?

Significantly, the OCR does not require local education agencies with a small number of language-minority students to institute formal remediation procedures and programs. However, the Equal Educational Opportunity Act, as interpreted by various federal courts, indicates the need to address the language needs of any individual who is denied equal educational opportunity due to a language barrier.

No Child Left Behind Act

The English Language Proficiency and Academic Achievement Act (Title III of the No Child Left Behind Act of 2001) consolidated the Bilingual Education Act with the Emergency Immigrant Education Program, transforming previous law to focus existing programs on teaching English to limited-English-proficient children, including immigrant children and youth, and expediting their transition to mainstream education classes.

Besides renaming the Office of Bilingual Education and Minority Languages Affairs as the Office of Educational Services for Limited English Proficient Children, Title III of the No Child Left Behind Act of 2001 has drastically changed the provisions for grants serving limited-English-proficient students. In general, states will have more chances to obtain grant money to educate limited-English-proficient students but will have lost the opportunity to use a student's native language beyond three years.

According to Congress, the primary goals of Title III are to increase the knowledge and use of English among limited-English-proficient children, to increase graduation rates among limited-English-proficient children, and to prepare students for transition as soon as possible into classrooms where instruction is not tailored for limited-English-proficient children. States can now request grant money to provide assistance to limited-English-proficient children who are using English, not just their native language.

In the spirit of spending more money at the local level, states must distribute at least 95% of their block grants to eligible education agencies to provide assistance to limited-English-proficient children. However, eligible entities are able to choose the method of instruction to teach limited-English-proficient children. Title III eliminates the previous requirement that 75% of funding be used to support programs using a child's native language for instruction.

To ensure a fair distribution of grant money, small states are guaranteed at least $500,000 under the grant program formula. An additional guarantee is that the allotment of funds will not be affected by the method of instruction employed in the language remediation programs in use in the state. Title III grants are awarded according to a formula based 80% on the number of limited-English-proficient children in the state and 20% on the number of immigrant children and youth in the state. This information is taken from the U.S. Census for the first two years. After this time, the data will come from the number of students being assessed for English proficiency in a state or data from the American Community Survey, which is available from the Department of Commerce, whichever the Department of Education determines to be the most accurate.

States must develop, and subsequently will be held accountable for, annual, measurable, achievement objectives to monitor the progress of LEP students in attaining English proficiency. Furthermore, school districts are required to notify parents of a program's failure to meet such achievement objectives for two years. After four years of failing to meet the achievement objectives, the state must require the school district to restructure its curriculum, program, and method of instruction. Specifically, Title III requires school districts receiving grant awards to complete an evaluation every year on the progress students are making toward learning English and achieving the same high levels of academic achievement as other students.

RESOURCES

Anstrom, K. "Defining the Limited-English-Proficient Student Population." *Directions in Language and Education* 1 (Summer 1996).

August, D., and Garcia, E. *Language Minority Education in the United States: Research, Policy, and Practice.* Springfield, Ill.: C.C. Thomas, 1988.

August, D., and Hakuta, K., eds. *Improving Schooling for Language-Minority Children: A Research Agenda.* Washington, D.C.: National Research Council, National Academy Press, 1997.

Blanco, G. "The Implementation of Bilingual-Bicultural Programs in the United States." In *Case Studies in Bilingual Education*, edited by B. Spolsky. Rowley, Mass.: Newbury House, 1978.

Cohen, M.; Berring, R.; and Olson, K. *Finding the Law.* St. Paul: West, 1989.

Corbett, D.D.; Dawson, J.L.; and Firestone, W.A. *School Context and School Change.* New York: Teachers College Press, 1984.

Crawford, J. *Bilingual Education: History, Politics, Theory, and Practice.* Trenton, N.J.: Crane, 1995.

Fleischman, H.L., and Hopstock, P.J. *Descriptive Study of Services to Limited-English Proficient Students, Volume 1: Summary of Findings and Conclusions.* Arlington, Va.: U.S. Department of Education, Development Associates, 1993.

Fradd, S.H., and Tikunoff, W.J. *Bilingual Education and Bilingual Special Education: A Guide for Administrators.* Boston: College-Hill, 1987.

Goldstein, S.; Gee, E.; and Daniel, P. *Law and Public Education.* 3rd ed. Charlottesville, Va.: Michie, 1995.

Goodlad, J. *What Schools Are For.* Bloomington, Ind.: Phi Delta Kappa Educational Foundation, 1979.

Jacobson, L. "Hispanic Children Outnumber Young Blacks for First Time." *Education Week*, 5 August 1998. http://www.edweek.org.

Jacobstein, J.M., and Mersky, R.M. *Fundamentals of Legal Research.* Mineola, N.Y.: Foundation Press, 1977.

Krashen, S. *Condemned Without a Trial: Bogus Arguments Against Bilingual Education*. Portsmouth, N.H.: Heinemann, 1999.

La Morte, M. *School Law: Cases and Concepts*. Englewood Cliffs, N.J.: Prentice-Hall, 1990.

Macias, R.F. *Summary Report of the Survey of the States' Limited-English Proficient Students and Available Educational Programs and Services, 1996-1997*. Washington, D.C.: National Clearinghouse for Bilingual Education, 1998. http://www.ncela.gwu.edu/ncbepubs/seareports/96-97/index.htm

McArthur, E.K. *Language Characteristics and Schooling in the United States: A Changing Picture, 1979 and 1989*. National Center for Education Statistics Doc. No. NCES 93-699. Washington, D.C.: U.S. Government Printing Office, 1993.

Miramontes, O.; Nadeau, A.; and Commins, N. *Restructuring Schools for Linguistic Diversity: Linking Decision-Making to Effective Programs*. New York: Teachers College Press, 1997.

Ovando, C.J., and Collier, V.P. *Bilingual and ESL Classrooms: Teaching in Multicultural Contexts*. New York: McGraw-Hill, 1985.

Piatt, B. *¿Only English? Law and Language Policy in the United States*. Albuquerque: University of New Mexico Press, 1990.

Samway, K., and McKeon, D. *Myths and Realities: Best Practices for Language-Minority Students*. Portsmouth, N.H.: Heinemann, 1999.

Schiffman, H. *Linguistic Culture and Language Policy*. New York: Routledge, 1996.

Soto, L. *Language, Culture, and Power*. Albany: State University of New York Press, 1997.

Statsky, W., and Wernet, J. *Case Analysis and Fundamentals of Legal Writing*. 4th ed. St. Paul, Minn.: West, 1995.

Stein, C.B. *Sink or Swim: The Politics of Bilingual Education*. New York: Praeger, 1986.

U.S. Census Bureau. *Language Spoken at Home and Ability to Speak English for United States, Regions and States: 1990*. CPH-L-133. Washington, D.C., 1993.

U.S. General Accounting Office (GAO). *Limited English Proficiency: A Growing and Costly Educational Challenge Facing Many School Districts*. GAO/HEHS-94-38. Washington, D.C.: U.S. Government Printing Office, 1994.

INDEX OF CASES
AND RELATED LEGISLATION AND REGULATIONS

Alvarado v. El Paso ISD, 426 F.Supp. 575 (W.D. Tex. 1976): 37-38, 102

Amos v. Board of School Directors of City of Milwaukee, 408 F. Supp. 765 (E.D. Wis. 1976): 38-39

Armstrong v. O'Connell, 74 F.R.D. 429 (E.D. Wis. 1977): 38-40, 107

Arvizu v. Waco Independent School District, 373 F. Supp. 1264 (W.D. Tex. 1973): 28-29, 102

Aspira v. Board of Education of the City of New York, 423 F. Supp. 647 (S.D.N.Y. 1976): 36-37, 106

Bartels v. Iowa, 262 U.S. 404 (1923): 27-28

Bishop v. Aronov, 926 F.2d 1066 (11th Cir. 1991): 86

California Teachers Association v. Davis, 64 F. Supp. 2d 945 (C.D. Cal. 1999): 85-87, 105

Cassell v. Texas, 339 U.S. 282 (1950): 5, 80

Castañeda v. Pickard, 648 F.2d 989 (5th Cir. 1981), aff'd, 781 F.2d 456 (1986): 8, 10, 12, 13-16, 22, 59-64, 67, 75-77, 78, 81, 89, 90, 93, 103, 105, 108, 110

Cintron v. Brentwood Union Free Sch. Dist., 455 F. Supp. 57 (E.D. N.Y. 1978): 40-43, 81, 106

Cisneros v. Corpus Christi Independent School District, 467 F.2d 142 (5th Cir. 1972): 28

Deerfield v. Ipswich Board of Education, 468 F. Supp. 1219 (N.D. S.D. 1979): 46-48, 104, 106-107

Evans v. Buchanan, 512 F. Supp. 839 (D. Del. 1981): 57-58, 106

Gomez v. Illinois State Board of Education, 614 F. Supp. 342 (N.D. Ill. 1985), aff'd, 811 F.2d 1030 (7th Cir. 1987): 8, 71-73, 90, 107

Guadalupe Org. Inc. v. Tempe Elem. Sch. Dist., 587 F.2d 1022 (9th Cir. 1978): 8, 44-46, 64-65, 90, 103

Heavy Runner v. Bremner, 522 F. Supp. 162 (D. Mont. 1981): 7, 64-65, 70, 104

Idaho Migrant Council v. Board of Education, 647 F.2d 69 (9th Cir.

1981): 58-59, 72, 104

In re Alien Children Education Litigation, 501 F. Supp. 544 (S.D. Tex. 1980): 8, 50-52, 103

Keyes v. School District No.1, Denver, Colorado, 413 U.S.189 (D. Colo. 1973), remanded, 521 F.2d 465 (10th Cir. 1975), 540 F. Supp. 399 (D. Colo. 1982), 576 F. Supp. 1503 (D. Colo. 1983): 9, 10, 35, 65-68, 108

Lau v. Nichols, 414 U.S. 563 (1974): 8, 9, 12, 19, 20-21, 29-31, 32, 34, 35, 36, 37, 46, 62, 64, 67, 70, 92, 102, 104, 108, 109

Lorain NAACP v. Lorain Board of Education, 768 F. Supp.1224 (N.D. Ohio, 1991), rev'd. 979 F.2d 1141 (6th Cir. 1992): 80-81, 107

Martin Luther King Jr. Elementary School Children et al. v. Ann Arbor School District, 73 F. Supp. 1371 (E.D. Mich. 1979): 9, 48-50, 106

Meyer v. Nebraska, 262 U.S. 390 (1923): 7, 18, 25-27

Morales v. Turman, 383 F. Supp. 53 (E.D. Tex. 1974): 103

Northwest Arctic School District v. Califano, No. A-77-216 (D. Alaska, Sept. 29,1978): 21

OHA v. DOE, 951 F. Supp. 1484 (D. Hawaii 1996): 8, 82-85, 93, 109

Otero v. Mesa, 408 F. Supp. 162 (D. Colo. 1975): 8, 34-36, 108

People Who Care v. Rockford Board of Education, 851 F. Supp. 905, (N.D. Ill. 1994): 8, 9, 10, 77-81, 107

Plyler v. Doe, 457 U.S. 202 (1982): 8, 52

Ray M. v. Board of Education, 884 F.Supp. 669 (E.D. N.Y. 1995): 81-82, 106

Rios v. Read, 480 F. Supp. 14 (E.D. N.Y. 1978): 43-44, 106

San Antonio Independent School District v. Rodriguez, 411 U.S. 1 (1973): 8, 45, 48, 66, 103, 108

Serna v. Portales Municipal Schs., 499 F.2d 1147 (10th Cir. 1974): 31-33, 35, 46, 67, 70, 103, 104, 108

Tangipahoa Parrish School Board v. U.S. Department of Education, 821 F.2d 1022 (5th Cir. 1987): 73-74

Teresa P. v. Berkeley Unified School District, 724 F. Supp. 698 (N.D. Cal. 1989): 9, 75-77, 104

United States v. Board of Education of the City of Chicago, 642 F. Supp. 206 (D. Ill. 1986): 68-70, 107

United States v. School District of Ferndale, Michigan, 577 F.2d 1339 (6th Cir. 1978): 64, 70, 104

United States v. Texas, 321 F.Supp. 1043 (E.D. Tex. 1970), 342 F. Supp. 24 (E.D. Tex. 1971), aff'd, 466 F.2d 518 (5th Cir. 1972), 506

F. Supp. 405 (1981), rev'd, 680 F.2d 356 (1982): 8, 34, 53-57, 103, 107
United States v. Texas Education Agency, 467 F.2d 848 (5th Cir. 1972): 39
United States v. Yonkers Board of Education, 624 F. Supp. 1276 (S.D. N.Y. 1985): 78
Regents of the University of California v. Bakke, 438 U.S. 265 (1978): 62
Valeria v. Wilson, 307 F.3d 1036 (9th Cir. 2002): 9, 87-90, 104-105
Washington v. Davis, 426 U.S. 229 (1976): 9, 62, 89, 103

Related Legislation and Regulations

Bilingual and Special Language Programs Act of Texas, S.B. 477, 1981: 53, 54.
Civil Rights Act of 1964, 42 U.S.C. §601 et. seq. (1964): 9, 18, 19-21, 24, 29, 30, 32, 37, 40-42, 43, 45, 46, 53, 54, 55, 57, 58-59, 62, 65-66, 71, 72, 75, 89-90, 91-92, 102, 103, 104, 105, 108, 109.
Equal Educational Opportunity Act of 1974, 20 U.S.C. §1701 et. seq. (1974): 7, 8, 10, 13, 18, 21-22, 24, 31, 40-42, 45, 46, 48, 50, 53, 54, 56, 57, 58, 50-64, 65-67, 70, 71, 72-73, 75-77, 88-89, 92-93, 103, 104, 105, 106-107, 108, 109, 110, 111.
Improving America's Schools Act, Title VII. Bilingual Education, Language Enhancement, and Language Acquisition Programs, 20 U.S.C. §7401 et. seq (1994): 19, 41-42, 52, 59-60, 73-74, 90, 94, 105.
Individuals with Disabilities Education Act (IDEA), 20 U.S.C. §1414 et. seq. (1997): 9, 34, 82, 93-94, 109.
Native American Language Act, 25 U.S.C. §2900 et. seq. (1990): 24, 82-85, 93, 108-109.
No Child Left Behind Act of 2001. Title III. English Language Proficiency and Academic Achievement Act. Public Law 107-110 (2001): 8, 9, 10, 14, 19, 24, 94-99, 107, 111-112.
Nondiscrimination Under Programs Receiving Federal Assistance Through the Department of Education, 34 C.F.R. §100.3 (1980): 20, 92.
Office of Civil Rights, May 1970 Memorandum. Identification of Discrimination and Denial of Services on the Basis of National Origin, 35 Fed. Reg. 11595 (1970): 8, 10, 11, 12, 20, 30, 92, 109-110.

Office of Civil Rights, U.S. Department of Education. "Office for Civil Rights Policy Regarding the Treatment of National Origin Minority Students Who Are Limited-English Proficient." [Online Memorandum]. 1990. Available: http://www.ed.gov.offices/OCR: 8, 10.

Office of Civil Rights, U.S. Department of Education. "Policy Update on School's Obligations Toward National Origin Minority Students with Limited-English Proficiency (LEP Students)." [Online Memorandum]. 1991. Available: http://www.ed.gov.offices/OCR: 8, 10, 11, 12, 13, 109-110.

Office of Civil Rights, U.S. Department of Education. "Provision of an Equal Education Opportunity to Limited-English Proficient Students." [On-line Brochure]. 2000. Available: http://www.ed.gov.offices/OCR: 8, 10, 110-111.

Title I: Helping Disadvantaged Children Meet High Standards, 34 C.F.R. §200.3 (1999).

ABOUT THE AUTHOR

Dr. Michael S. Mills is a full-time teacher at Sheridan High School, a school district 30 miles south of Little Rock, Arkansas. Dr. Mills earned his B.A. and M.Ed. from Louisiana Tech University and his Ed.D. from the University of Arkansas at Little Rock, where he serves as adjunct instructor, teaching educational leadership courses in curriculum and current events.